89345662 ✗

D1562892

The Challenges of Gifted Children

The Challenges of Gifted Children

EMPOWERING PARENTS TO MAXIMIZE THEIR CHILD'S POTENTIAL

Barbara Klein

Foreword by John D. McNeil

RARITAN VALLEY COMMUNITY COLLEGE
EVELYN S. FIELD LIBRARY

PRAEGER ™

An Imprint of ABC-CLIO, LLC
Santa Barbara, California • Denver, Colorado

Copyright © 2015 by Barbara Klein

All rights reserved. No part of this publication may be reproduced, stored in a retrieval system, or transmitted, in any form or by any means, electronic, mechanical, photocopying, recording, or otherwise, except for the inclusion of brief quotations in a review, without prior permission in writing from the publisher.

Library of Congress Cataloging-in-Publication Data

Klein, Barbara Schave.
    The challenges of gifted children : empowering parents to maximize their child's potential / Barbara Klein ; foreword by John D. McNeil.
        pages cm
    Includes bibliographical references and index.
    ISBN 978–1–4408–3338–0 (hard copy : alk. paper) — ISBN 978–1–4408–3339–7 (ebook)
1. Gifted children. 2. Child rearing. 3. Parent and child. I. Title.
HQ773.5.K538   2015
649'.155—dc23   2015015703

ISBN: 978–1–4408–3338–0
EISBN: 978–1–4408–3339–7

19 18 17 16 15   1 2 3 4 5

This book is also available on the World Wide Web as an eBook.
Visit www.abc-clio.com for details.

Praeger
An Imprint of ABC-CLIO, LLC

ABC-CLIO, LLC
130 Cremona Drive, P.O. Box 1911
Santa Barbara, California 93116-1911

This book is printed on acid-free paper ∞

Manufactured in the United States of America

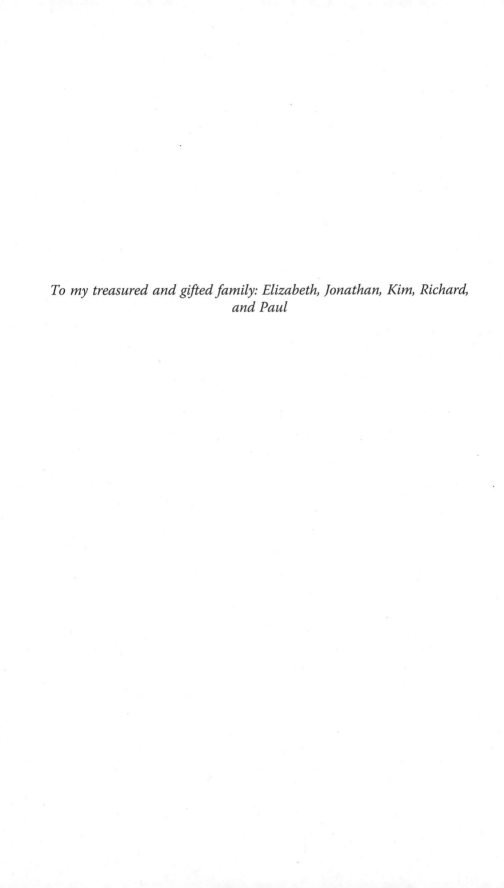

To my treasured and gifted family: Elizabeth, Jonathan, Kim, Richard, and Paul

Contents

Foreword

The author of *The Challenges of Gifted Children*, Dr. Barbara Klein, is acclaimed both for her specialized knowledge of giftedness—scholarship, research, teaching, writing—and her extraordinary successful therapeutic counseling of gifted children and their parents. In this book, she brings to life the voices of gifted children, illuminating new insights into their special strengths and developmental needs. Further, the author presents accounts and case studies from parents of these children that reveal unique concerns parents have when their child is gifted. Noteworthy is Klein's effective uncovering of the issues thwarting child and parent and her engagement of them in ways that overcome developmental blocks, replacing parental uncertainty and despair with a new confidence.

Beyond the gifted and their parents, others will profit greatly, as child and parent adhere to the understandings and practices delineated in CGC. Enhanced domestic relations and quality of family life for all, for example, are common outcomes for those receiving Klein's guidance for the gifted.

The Challenges of Gifted Children casts about for a big net of readers. In addition to new understandings of the nature of giftedness and the enhancement of talent, parents of gifted and nongifted alike while reading CGC, will be led to re-examine their motives and roles in parenting, bringing to bear new cautions and insights underlying this old question: Am I trying to make another like me when one is enough?

Teachers will learn how to identify and understand their gifted students—emotionally, intellectually, socially, academically—learning how to both address their exceptionality and contribute to the enrichment of the class.

In reading this book, school leaders and reformers will become aware of the deficiencies in schooling of the gifted as well as the emergence of innovative departures based on new understandings of the gifted in relation to school safety, acceleration, individualism, and the importance of social skills. Although Klein emphasizes parental care in selecting the right school for one's gifted child, and subsequently parental participation in school life, she shows how schools, in becoming right schools for the gifted, can become better schools for all.

This book is a comprehensive but readable text with scope for readers to connect with their own concerns. A spouse will draw a partner's attention to a particular revelation. A mother or grandmother will want the other to read the section that speaks directly to issues affecting the guidance she wants to provide her gifted child. Although the author is an expert on giftedness and experienced in overcoming obstacles to its promise, she offers respectful but firm treatment for the gifted and their caregivers.

John D. McNeil, Professor Emeritus
Graduate School of Education & Information Studies,
University of California–Los Angeles (UCLA)

Acknowledgments

Paul Macirowski, my soulmate and writing partner/editor, helped me through the entire process of writing *The Challenges of Gifted Children: Empowering Parents to Maximize Their Child's Potential.*

Paul's wisdom, sensitivity, and commitment to working with me and the many families with gifted children who consult me, has sustained me through good times and trying, as well as discouraging times that were involved in writing this book.

I am grateful and appreciative to the parents who have consulted with me and shared their thoughts and feelings with me in words and in writing. Their ideas and opinions make my new book more meaningful and accessible to my reader.

Joelle List helped me with typing and preparing the manuscript efficiently and accurately. Her assistance and positive attitude were valuable as I worked to complete this book.

Johanna Keogh and Daniella Batsheva worked with me to design the jacket cover with seriousness and grace. They were open to my ideas and tried to communicate them in drawings to the marketing department. I appreciate their time and effort of my behalf.

Lastly, but not *leastly*, I am grateful to all of the children who have come to play with me and share their excitement and concerns. Asynchronous development was again and again brought to life by these special and precocious children, whose gifts I hope will make this world a better place in which to thrive.

Introduction

Dealing with the high points of giftedness—discovery, insights, and prestige—and the low points—despair, darkness, and feelings of failure—has punctuated my personal and professional life. My deep curiosity about what it "really" means to be a successful gifted person began in childhood. As a six-year-old, I was not thinking about giftedness from an artistic, academic, or clinical perspective, but I did wonder why my mother thought my older brother Alan was a genius. Alan attended the special "opportunity" classes at Rosewood Avenue School in West Hollywood. My twin sister Marjorie and I went only to the regular classes, happily, without any envy for what our brother was learning. We wondered about what was such an opportunity in his classroom.

But more strange and unusual events occurred because our brother had unquenchable interests in outer space that Marjorie and I found unique and also entertaining. Alan was always building rocket ships with his friends in our back yard. And once we went as a family with his friends to the Mojave Desert to watch him launch his rocket ship. I remember my sister and I sitting in the sand trying really hard not to get sand in our peanut butter and jelly sandwiches. We were six and enjoyed the adventure.

Little did we know that someday in the future our brother would launch his solar experiments into outer space. His cameras, which went along with his solar experiments, took 20 years to construct at NASA. But the cameras did not work because his research team had difficulty simulating the atmosphere in space. Our brother talked with the astronauts, who were circling our planet, about the outcomes of his research. Together, Alan and the astronauts wrote a failure analysis of the project and of course, began again. Thinking about how my brother's interest in the sun and outer space had such a profound impact on solar physics and space travel still boggles my mind. Alan's success as a world famous astrophysicist is amazing. Go, Alan!

Growing up, my identical twin and I saw different aspects of the problem of living with a genius. We—my sister and I—were not smart. We were second tier in importance. Our brother was "weird." And he had weird friends who were not very talkative. Actually, they were very involved with their slide rulers. We wondered who they played with at recess and lunch. Did they have interests other than the best cars ever made? Why was mathematics so easy for Alan and his friends? Today, mental health professionals would label some of these children as being on the autism spectrum or having Asperger syndrome.

In the 1950s, very little was known about the psychological issues of gifted children. Marjorie and I worried that our brother would never find a woman who could relate to him. But he did. Alan married another astrophysicist who studied black holes, while my twin and I pursued liberal arts educations at UC Berkeley. After seeing Alan have a childhood of scientific clarity that was totally black and white and lacking in any understanding of the importance of feelings, my sister and I launched into understanding interpersonal relationships at college. (This passion to understand what motivates others toward healthy relationships is still important to my sense of self and my professional life.)

My twin and I finally settled in separate cities and started our own families. My life went on. I married and had two children. I was determined to raise my children with minds of their own and an abundance of social skills. I did not totally throw out the idea of giftedness. I wanted to raise my children to love learning and to appreciate the struggles of others. Luckily for Richard and Elizabeth, they attended Crossroads School in Santa Monica, where they had devoted and brilliant teachers; very curious, creative, kind, and caring friends; and overall high-quality educational experiences. Rigid social interactions were not a part of my children's childhood and teenage years. I was always concerned about shades of gray, how they were feeling, and what they were thinking.

When my kids were old enough, I went back to graduate school. And the other mothers took tennis lessons. I began to feel like an outsider in the world of parents. But I never considered myself as gifted. I was always surprised when I came in in first place as an undergraduate or graduate student. Really, I was just intent on developing an academic and clinical understanding of child development. Completing a doctorate in education and then another one in clinical psychology, I came to understand giftedness from a different perspective than I had seen it when I was "just" a sister or a parent. Another very important lesson I learned was that no one agreed on what giftedness really was, but everyone thought they were right. I trained in and practiced clinical psychology. Because of my background in education, I received countless referrals for psychological testing of children. I worked with the Mirman School for the Highly Gifted in Bel Air, California, doing IQ evaluations. I consulted with parents of gifted children about school placement. I started a parenting support group for mothers and fathers of gifted children to educate them about the social emotional issues that are unique to this population.

I wrote a parenting book, *Raising Gifted Kids: Everything You Need to Know to Help Your Exceptional Child Thrive*, in 2006. In this book, I focused on helping parents understand the importance of being a good enough parent. Since the publication of this book, I have received thousands of emails and phone calls from parents who want my opinion about their child's strange gifted behaviors. Parents bring their children to see me and ask, "Why are there so many dinosaurs, temper tantrums, friendship issues, so much separation anxiety, and so much boredom at school?" Thinking about other parents' concerns, I saw a universal theme. Gifted children are a psychological challenge, and parents need to be educated, coached, and supported to raise them to achieve their potential. I am 100% positive that raising talented children is very difficult and stressful.

I understood from listening to parents who called for advice that educators need to know more about the challenges of nurturing talent. I finally understood my mother's total overindulgence of my brother's intellectual passions. I began to respect her single-mindedness and determination to keep Alan's brain challenged. Her intensity was, on the other hand, possessed and inappropriate. Was mom a show-off or on the right track when she gave her son so much support, acknowledgement, and freedom? Were my sister and I really marginalized or damaged because we had to play second fiddle to our brother? My twin sister has had a successful career as an author and a professor at Stanford. I have had an exciting life writing and working with families. I ask myself, "Was mother actually right, given what knowledge she had about raising a gifted child?" These thoughts often torment me and have spurred my interest in understanding how to deal with the challenges that parents face when working to develop their child's potential.

My knowledge, professional and personal experiences, and opinions are explained in the book you have before you: *The Challenges of Gifted Children: Empowering Parents to Optimize Their Child's Potential.* Chapter 1 begins by explaining that giftedness is often handed from parent to child. A true gift is innate and cannot be developed or trained. Gifts need to be nurtured. Definitions of giftedness vary, as does giftedness itself, because talent manifests in different ways in each individual. Academics, educators, clinical psychologists, and parents all have different ways of assessing special intensity, passion, and talent in the children they are concerned about or working with. How to put the different perspectives on giftedness together and decide what is important for parents, teachers, administrators, and close family to understand is the focus of Chapter 1.

Chapter 2 details parents' role in developing giftedness to its truest potential. I explain that good enough parents or non-narcissistically invested parents are taking the right approach with gifted children because of the child's deep perfectionist identity. Overidentification with one's infant or child is a form of enmeshment that creates psychological boundary issues for parents and children. Examples to support my ideas are illustrated using the words and thoughts of parents who have attended my parenting groups or consulted with me. Strategies that help keep clear the difference between your child's intensity and your own intensity are presented.

Chapter 3 discusses why setting limits and managing discipline is different and difficult with gifted children. Strategies to help parents make important decisions about discipline are included, along with the personal struggles that parents talk about when they have to set limits.

Chapter 4 describes the intensity of the gifted child. Overexcitability and intensity are part of the gifted person's personality. As smart as an individual may be is as intense and excitable as he or she can be in provocative situations. This chapter explains different types of intensities and how to navigate the home and school landscape with this knowledge in hand. Parental reactions to their children's emotional intensity and advice are presented

Chapter 5 explains the common learning problems that gifted kids have to learn to deal with and how parents can support these efforts. Learning highs and lows—asynchronous development—form the basis of learning challenges. Parents need to assess the strengths and limitations of their children and meet them at the top of their curiosity and on their level of struggle. Social and emotional issues surface from the child's uneven development. Proactive strategies that lead to solutions will be suggested.

Chapter 6 discusses how to find the right school for your child and family. There is no one school that will meet the needs of all gifted children. Perhaps the most frustrating problem parents face is finding a school that will meet their child's and their family's needs. Seeing education as an important investment in your child's future, I approach the issue of finding the right school in a manner similar to investing in the stock market. I suggest the top (most important) questions to ask at interviews and how you can get beyond marketing materials. After you read this chapter, you will be prepared to make a good decision about where your child will most likely thrive.

Chapter 7 describes contemporary issues such as bullying, overuse of video games, over- and underachievement, sibling rivalry, family stress, and existential depression that parents may face every day with their spirited and intense son or daughter. Parenting traps special to this unique group of parents are described along with suggestions to avoid being stymied by others.

Chapter 8 gives strategies to empower parents to come up with their own solutions to the most critical challenges of gifted children.

1

Giftedness Is the Child's Legacy

THE CHALLENGES OF DEFINING GIFTEDNESS

"How can I know if my child is gifted?" is usually the first question parents ask when they consult with me about how to understand and parent their precocious child. More sensitive issues are rarely brought up at an initial consultation. Whether mothers and fathers are ashamed or in denial, they are reluctant to share their concerns that they think their child may be hyperactive, learning disabled, on the autistic spectrum, or suffering with emotional issues related to inadequate parenting. In my experience, parents who get in touch with me actually know the answer is "yes" to their question, "Is my child gifted?" Parents know because they are extremely smart and have gone through the psychological problems associated with being gifted themselves. Gifted parents can see the signs. Actually, most parents who want to consult with me have precocious children with "normal" emotional and behavioral issues.

Problems with school placement and home management issues that are hard to understand and to contain are the focus at the beginning of working out how to deal with the challenges of a gifted child. What goes into a working strategy to deal with a gifted child's development depends on how concerned parents are about getting their parenting strategies in order. Some parents just need to know the facts. The score on an IQ test or some other form of confirmation allows them to know the reality that they have a gifted child. They are not curious about what it means to their child's future and to how they will parent. While some parents take their time to understand what approach will work the best with their child, in actuality, it takes time to understand your child's score. There are always hurdles to jump over. The length of time and the intensity of the problem the gifted child is having can in serious situations lead to the need for psychotherapy and even medication.

Obviously, the reality that educators, psychologists, and academicians cannot agree on a definition of giftedness understandably makes parents confused. Still, I am not sure why the question of "is my child gifted" becomes such a pivotal turning point for parental concern and action. From my experiences working with families, I know that identification of giftedness comes from a personal sensibility of a parent or teacher or a well done psychological evaluation. I will still restate my understanding of the definitions of giftedness just to make sure that I am on the same page as my reader. I believe that the uniqueness of a "gift" cannot be defined objectively, in exact words or measures, and then compared with other gifts in other individuals who are gifted. The personal and subjective nature of giftedness is often elusive and hard to define. Obviously, there is no one definition of giftedness, which creates confusion for everyone who is involved with raising and educating a gifted child. In general, educators and mental health professionals are far too undereducated and underinformed to understand the emotional and behavioral uniqueness of the gifted child.

I believe from my strong knowledge base and clinical experiences with bright and intense children that a gift is something that is handed down to the child from his or her parents. There is definitely a genetic component to unique talent. My understanding, or point of view, may seem to have elitist tones for those readers who are of the belief that every child can be seen as gifted. Absolutely, there are invisible and hidden gifted people whose parents cannot see their potential. It is entirely reasonable and imperative that psychologists and educators try to ask questions that will identify the signs of the invisible gifted person.[1]

On the other hand, the reality is that giftedness is hard to nurture and is never an easy problem for parents to deal with. Parents I work with can spend time wishing their child were normal, not gifted. So there is some irony to the whole confusion about the true and exact definition of giftedness. Scholarly books are written in an academic tone on conceptions of giftedness.[2] Academic and clinical identification are not of great interest to parents who are in the hot seat trying to raise their gifted child or to teachers or therapists who want to help the child and parent.

MYTHS AND MISINFORMATION ABOUT GIFTED KIDS DISTRACT AND CONFUSE PARENTS, TEACHERS, AND MENTAL HEALTH PROFESSIONALS

Myths about how gifted children are perceived and endorsed by our society complicate the identification of, interest in, and acceptance of gifted children.[3] What comes to my mind first and actually still makes me feel uncomfortable is the idea that gifted children are "nerds." Thinking personally, and even if I am a nerd, I don't want to see myself is this unflattering light. "Labels" are bad for everyone because of their reductionist nature. And so I imagine that this slur makes other most likely nerds feel awkward. Unfortunately for our children and the future of our society, seeing unique abilities as "strange" is seriously harmful and destructive. Making the unique talents of gifted individuals highly revered and nurtured is definitely not in our mindset as a culture. If our culture is to overcome disparaging comments about genius, parents, educators, and mental health professionals have to make a difference by understanding their children's special abilities and work toward debunking the myth of the nerd.

Other myths that grow out of the new equality trend that is supposedly nonbiased and nonelitist come to my mind, such as "all children are gifted." While all children may be special gifts to their parents, emotionally intense and special intellectual, imaginational, and artistic abilities are very rare and unusual. The idea that all children are gifted is totally wrong and ridiculous as well. Giftedness involves a set of abilities and capacities that must be addressed and nurtured. Gifted individuals are complicated thinkers. They have a rich internal life that is very intense and can be explosive. Extremely bright individuals can become misfits in the everyday world. Clearly, not all children and adults are gifted.

Another dangerous myth that has grown out of the new trend of the "never enough parent" suggests that giftedness is not real. Rather, precociousness is just something that hot housing helicopter parents have thought up. This mythical idea makes parents question themselves inordinately. Undermining and shaming can be elicited in parents who are led to believe that they are just bragging about their child and their abilities as a parent. This myth alienates parents from their children's schools. The special needs of the gifted child easily fall by the wayside when giftedness is perceived as abilities that can be taught through drills and pressure.

The myth that gifted children must be and are easy to raise infuriates me. Jealous parents who wish they had a gifted child perpetuate this humiliating myth, which makes it harder for parents and educators to make allowances that precocious children need to develop their potential. Parents can become isolated and trapped by this serious misunderstanding. Parents says to me, "If it is so easy to raise a gifted kid, why am I feeling so lost and confused about how to be effective with my son?"

The myth that gifted children are strangely manipulative, a tad antisocial, and grow up to be white-collar criminals is as absurd as it sounds. And this myth can be amped up to a more seriously deranged version that gifted children become serial killers or unabombers. Biographies of gifted individuals and stories in the news paint the special drive of the prodigy in a dark and troubled light. While some geniuses are really quite involved in their own ideas and unable to relate to others, they are not necessarily potential criminals, homicidal, or destined to commit suicide. These myths that perpetuate the belief that giftedness is related to mental illness and antisocial behavior are naturally disturbing and confusing to parents who think their child might be gifted. In addition, teachers can react too negatively to strong-minded gifted children who are pegged as troublemakers as early as preschool and kindergarten because they draw violent pictures or have trouble making friends.

Old-fashioned rigid thinking from traditional educators about pressuring gifted children to perform at their highest abilities conflicts with what is really being understood by innovative gifted educators who have an entirely different opinion on what is in the best interests of the gifted child. Because gifted children are perfectionistic by nature, educational rigidity can intensify their self-critical behavior. Unfortunately, old-fashioned and traditional educational policies holds back innovation in curriculum development and instruction for gifted kids, leaving parents of gifted children alone to fend for themselves as they look to educate and develop their son's or daughter's potential.

Raising a gifted child is a challenge that can be disarming to all of the senses. Myths and general confusion about especially talented children and adults reinforce already existing barriers to further understanding and developing the potential resources of our gifted children. Parents and educators need to work diligently to debunk these myths and learn the best ways to advocate for gifted children who eventually become gifted adults who could make a difference to the well-being of others in our society.[4]

HOW IMPORTANT IS STANDARDIZED GIFTED TESTING OR A GIFTED EVALUATION?

It helped me to know my son's IQ score because it gave me perspective. When you wrote that Adam is in the 99.9%, then I knew just how different he really is. I needed help from a real expert since so few people have a child with his abilities. I won't ever tell my son his IQ but it helped me to convince my husband that he needed a different educational environment.

—*Alisa*

It has become easier for me to empathize with Jon's passionate and intense reactions to the world after Dr. Klein's evaluation and explanation of his asynchronous development. It makes sense that the gift of high level verbal ability and abstract reasoning presenting in a physically and emotionally immature child is hard to rectify. Understanding where Jon's struggles come from helps me to help him feel more comfortable at home and at school.

—*Rene*

Of course, a gifted evaluation is essential to understanding the structure of your son's or daughter's way of perceiving and reacting to his or her emotional and physical world. Giftedness comes in different varieties and flourishes in different ways. A child who reads early may have more difficulty with social interaction; a child who is very imaginative may have difficulty wanting to learn to read. Qualitative assessments that parents can complete or have completed by an observer are very useful tools that help us understand how the child prefers to relate to the world.[5] These subjective evaluations put in words the child's strengths and limitations. Teachers and parents gain insight and information from the reports that come from these assessments.

Psychologists are interested in individual differences between children and can often use intelligence tests, neurological tests, and other behavioral checklists to pick up emotional, social, and cognitive issues that reference or suggest extremely high abilities and talents. Projective testing can reveal underlying emotional issues that need to be addressed in psychotherapy.

One serious downfall of standardized psychological measures of intelligence can be the professional who administers the test. Unfortunately, most psychologists are not educated about the differences in testing gifted children and adults. And, of course, psychological testing is not available to all children. Unfortunately, because of lack of resources, standardized psychological measures are often called elitist by parents and school districts that cannot afford to do the testing. Psychological testing is still more predictive of general intellectual ability than achievement testing. Understandably, psychological testing does not predict who will become renowned because of the score that is attained on an IQ test.[6]

Psychologists who have experience with the gifted population can help parents understand their child's idiosyncrasies. Psychological definitions of giftedness include an IQ score in the 98th percentile or above on the Wechsler Scales or Stanford V. Twice exceptionality, which is giftedness coupled with a learning disability, attention deficit disorder, or the autistic spectrum disorder, can definitely be understood through the use of a wide battery of psychological and neurological tests coupled with behavioral checklists for parents and teachers.

Extremely high achievement on school-related testing is another clue of a child's giftedness. Public schools use achievement testing to identify gifted children, which is useful if the gifted child is a "schoolhouse" prodigy.[7] And the opposite is also true. It is not uncommon for gifted children to become underachievers due to a great interest in their imagination, intellect, creativity, perfectionism, and feelings that they are misunderstood at school. Some kids do not test well due to indifference or anxiety.[8]

In addition, children who are musical, artistic, athletic, or dramatic prodigies should be identified as gifted because their abilities are so high in comparison to the norm. Emotional intensity and intuitiveness are also a sign of precociousness. Using words and communicating with adults in a very mature dialogue or using complicated math skills signals that a child is capable of soaring to great heights.

BEHAVIORAL CHARACTERISTICS GIVE A BROADER PICTURE OF GIFTEDNESS

My extensive experiences working with gifted children lead me to believe that the phenomenological definition of giftedness, a definition based on observations of the individual, is most accurate and understandable. Observing gifted behavior in children and adults, one finds a greater sensitivity, awareness, and ability to transform and understand emotional and intellectual ideas and experiences. A heightened ability to understand inner experiences and to translate theses ideas into words and actions is another observable behavioral example of giftedness. A complexity of thought process, imagination, and sensation that is very different from the norm of children suggests that the individual may be a prodigy. In addition, there is an asynchronicity to precocious development.[9] Gifted children and adults can be very talented in one area and totally struggling in other areas of their development. Uneven development complicates how bright children and teenagers adjust and function in social situations and at school. Learning highs and lows are inevitable and a marker for giftedness. High and lows are observable and recordable on gifted evaluations.

A broad behavioral definition of giftedness includes a mixture of characteristics that vary from individual to individual. Some of the following behavioral tendencies are indicative of giftedness:[10]

1. An early and enduring passion for communication, which is seen in talking and demanding in infants, toddlers, and young children. In older children, adolescents, and adults there is a deep curiosity and profound interest in making sense of the world in intellectual, imaginative, and idealistic terms and talking to others about their ideas. Perhaps this is why dinosaurs and Star Wars characters are so fascinating for gifted kids, as these animals and imaginary characters give the child room to talk about the different aspects of their world by exploring fantasy worlds.
2. A remarkable capacity for concentration in areas of interest throughout life. Gifted individuals are project orientated, and getting them to stop what they are working on is extremely difficult at all stages of life.
3. Persistence in mastering a task that is developmentally advanced to their age and life stage. This persistent behavior makes transitions difficult to accept and can cause serious frustration at any stage of life. Whether understanding rock climbing, bullying, drawing, or reading, gifted individuals are relentless.

4. Emotional intensity in reaction to thoughts, feelings, and actions that needs to be understood and an outlet developed for their sensitivity. While this is a life-long issue, coping strategies need to be developed in childhood and worked out in relationships and career directions. There can be a great deal of shame related to emotional intensity because others may not understand where such strong feelings are coming from.

5. Perfectionism related to task completion and interpersonal authenticity—absolute attentiveness to emotional intensity—is a longstanding issue that needs to be understood and tamed. This perfectionistic behavior is seen in friendship disappointment, in tearing up homework or complaining that they can't do something well within their capability level.

6. Anxiety over separation and new situations in childhood, in adolescence, and in times of crisis throughout life. This vulnerability is temporary and dramatic.

7. A strong inclination toward insight and introspection throughout life that leads to profound questions about the meaning of life. Existential depression—the ultimate meaninglessness of life—can often torment gifted individuals.

8. Asynchronous development—learning highs and lows—in children and teen-agers. The resolution of the variability in strengths occurs with the development of coping strategies and maturity.

9. Issues with overachievement or underachievement throughout schooling and career that are often related to stressful life situations.

10. Socialization problems with same-age peers, especially in childhood and adolescence. Social skill development will need to be attended to through education and role modeling.

11. An ability to act older than they are and than they feel in childhood and adolescence. This characteristic confuses parents, teachers, and friends.

12. Thinking they can outsmart their parents and make up their own rules in childhood. Later in life, this grandiosity can affect interpersonal relationships or job security.

13. A tendency toward existential depression—a nongenetic sense of hopelessness—throughout life. Small children ask serious why questions such as "Where is God?" Teenagers can act out their desperation about the meaninglessness of life. Adults who are idealistic and hopeful are able to contain existential depression through artistic expression.

HOW PARENTS TALK ABOUT GIFTEDNESS

Parents have an entirely different outlook on giftedness than psychologists and educators. Effective and caring parents are concerned about how to deal with their child's intellectual, social, and emotional behavior, as well as their education. Mothers and fathers rarely have time to discuss the definitions of giftedness that are psychological, conceptual, or academic. Behavioral characteristics help parents understand who their precocious child is and what they especially need from them as parents. Parents' reaction and plan for their child is crucial to the development of their overall potential.[11] The lack of educational and emotional support for parents of gifted children coupled with the general misunderstanding about what it means to be gifted leave parents at a serious disadvantage. Parents want their children to flourish socially, intellectually, and creatively. Parents want their children to learn to interact with other children, teachers, and adults. Parents need help guiding their child.

Usually, but in unusual ways, parents who have worked with me react to the news that they have a gifted child in one of three ways:

1. *Accessory parent reactions.* Parents are overly enthusiastic—just plain delighted to be told that there is giftedness in their family. This information provides them with a new status symbol, another accessory to indicate their own brilliance and power. In other words, having a gifted child becomes a status symbol, just another priceless item to show off.
2. *Dreading parent reactions.* The family is living in denial and chooses to ignore the overwhelming and thus unwanted information that their child is gifted. For these types of families, other overriding family issues such as financial stress, divorce, or religious and cultural values shove the issue of giftedness to the back burner.
3. *Good enough reactions.* The most adaptive reaction is the concerned parent who is able to realize that they have been given a huge responsibility. Concerned parents want to do the best they can given their resources. This good enough reaction is of course the most adaptive and will be described later in this book.

I asked some of the parents I work with how they decided that their child was gifted. Here are some of their responses.

George, a prominent surgeon: *When Jacob was nine months old, he called the flowers in our garden bougainvilleas. I knew that his use of words was unusual. I began to think of our son as a gifted child.*

Laura, a college professor: *When David was 20 months old, he could name and categorize every kind of car by manufacturer. I was aware that his interests and memory were unusual. My son was demonstrating qualities of a gifted child.*

Mary, a writer: *Jake was a high-strung child who had to follow a strict routine throughout the day and at bedtime. He was shy at Mommy and Me group. When he started talking to me about black holes on the sun at the age of three, I realized he was a gifted child.*

Lisa, a human resource specialist: *Aidan can do any sport by just watching it being played by others. From the youngest age, he was ultra-aware of his body and what it could do. He leapt off rocks at 18 months old and landed like a gymnast; and he hit a tennis ball like a pro.*

Aidan loved telling stories with complex characters and adult vocabulary. He would describe battles between pirates and the love between two people.

He is still funny and can mimic comedians and create jokes and plays. Adian loves active science, physics, and chemistry.

Julie, an artist: *I think my child is gifted because. . .*
He does math in his head better than me.
He was the only child I ever knew who could read at age three and a half.
He remembers every insignificant detail.
He analyzes architecture and engineering unlike any of my friends' children.
He watches the science channel and understands it better than his father and I do.

Rhiannon, a film editor: *I think Meg is gifted because she is a very quick learner. She has an almost photographic memory and can learn a concept after just one or two explanations. She wants to learn things other children her age are not interested in such as anatomy and space science.*

Sandy, a homemaker: *I didn't realize my child was gifted until third grade. Out of curiosity, I read a book at the pediatrician's office on the misdiagnosis of ADHD in children and adults that opened my eyes to my son's giftedness. I always knew that Don was smart, but all parents think their child is smart. He could spell three-letter words at the age of two and write and illustrate long stories in kindergarten.*

Lynette, an art teacher: *It has taken me a while to use the* gifted *term and feel comfortable using it in relationship to my son. There were some clues along the way. When Carl was 17 months old, he had 60 birds memorized. We knew then that he was bright and able minded. We did not want to alienate other parents who might think we were bragging. We did not want him to be gifted and "abnormal"—an outlier. Now we realize that it is easier to have a gifted label, as it helps to understand what upsets him.*

PARENTING STYLE IS CRUCIAL TO GIFTED DEVELOPMENT

Curiosity about the development of the bright child is certainly widespread. Self-help books, gifted associations, websites, and parent support groups provide information and hands-on strategies for dealing with the often difficult to understand and contain smart child. Concerned parents of spirited, bright kids readily seek out "live" in-person advice and insight from professionals to help them feel more competent about their parenting skills. In contrast, very little has been written about what is unique about the devoted, high-achieving, bright, and gifted parents who strive to give their children rich intellectual and creative opportunities that will afford them better lives than they themselves experienced. If you are wondering why understanding and emotional support for parents is often a top-secret priority, consider these thoughts based on my experiences working with gifted parents who have challenging, intense children:

1. Gifted parents are intense and perfectionistic. When they have to admit that they are having problems with their gifted child, they often feel ashamed of themselves. Unfortunately, gifted parents feel too proud when they supposedly do "right" for their son or daughter. Feeling like they are making mistakes and feeling inadequate is very stressful and confusing. With their simplistic and rigid perfectionistic thinking, these perfectionistic parents have difficulty understanding the problems. The most common phone call or email I get from these intensely perfectionistic parents goes like this:

   Hello Dr. Klein, I am looking for help to find a school for my son or daughter, who I believe may be gifted. At least that is what the kindergarten teacher was suggesting at our conference about John. As well, my parents are encouraging us to get help in learning to set limits. My dad says we need to be strict with John or we will be sorry later. I wish I could figure this out by myself, but I am stuck. Can you get back to me?

   Hello Dr. Klein, I am having problems getting my preschooler to let me leave her at day care. Her teacher thinks she is really smart and sensitive. My daughter's curiosity is truly remarkable, but she does have a hard time connecting with other children. Allison prefers to go and read or play with the large lizards in the science center. We don't want to brag about Allison. We are not those kind of parents. Can you do a gifted evaluation?

   These initial types of phone calls and emails reflect the parent's uncomfortable feelings about reaching out for help because help is a reflection of inadequacy or senseless bragging. Carefully, these anxious and self-critical parents focus on school issues or teachers' or grandparents' concerns. Deeper behavioral and self-esteem issues arise as the family comes to understand the range of their son's or daughter's gifted issues. Parents become more aware of the complexity of their role of nurturing their intense child.

2. Gifted parents often believe deep down inside of themselves that other parents and teachers will judge them negatively. Self-critical parents are quick to blame themselves. Far too many parents say that they imagine I will believe they are slightly crazy and that is why they are having problems parenting their precocious son or daughter. These phone calls and emails reflect their deep insecurities and their limited way of assessing their problems as a parent.

   Parents of gifted children are often very introspective and perfectionistic like their children. Getting a realistic sense of what is wrong with their child can become too troubling for them; they can become frozen in their own self-loathing.

   Hi Dr. Klein, I was so happy to read what you have written on your website about gifted children. Some days I feel like I have made so many mistakes and that I have simply ruined my child's life by being too strict or not strict enough. If I was less confused about how to parent my child, our family life would run more smoothly. Or rather it wouldn't be a chaotic mess. Can you help me?

Hi Dr. Klein, Please call me, my best friend says you have helped her with her kids who are really little terrors like my children. I have already made so many mistakes. I am so ineffective. I need someone to do damage control. Can you help me?

Phone contact or email contact from these more obviously honest, self-blaming parents clearly reflects the ongoing drama in the family. While insight into emotional issues is very useful for developing strategies to nourish the child's gifted potential, it can also reflect an inability of the parent to take his or her problems seriously from a practical point of view. Making a plan with these types of parents can be extremely difficult. In other words, talking the talk is not walking the right path and should not be confused with making serious plans and sitting limits that come from parental ideas and insight.

3. Gifted parents, who are serious overachievers, think that if they try harder, they will make the right decisions someday. Eventually, however, they get to the end of their ropes, and they call me and say something like this:

   Dr. Klein, I just got a call from my son and the principal. Jason is being bullied at school. We have taught him everything we can about how to handle bullying, but he refuses to go back to the classroom. A bully just drew a picture of a penis on his notebook when he was in the bathroom. My son is so humiliated that he can't face his classmates. I have tried everything I can think of to help my son do well in school, and nothing has worked. Do you have any new ideas?

   Dr. Klein, can you call me back? My daughter is in the best gifted school in our community. We moved here because they have the best schools. Now, she loves to go to school. Her tutor is helping her express herself intellectually. As a family, we still have problems. Annabel will not go anywhere with us as a family if she does not know what to expect. She can be so anxious that her behavior disrupts the entire family. We just end up staying home to avoid Annabel's temper tantrums.

Overachiever phone calls are very common from the never say die population of gifted parents. What is so interesting about this frenzied group of parents is that they are totally blind to how hard they have worked to solve their kids' issues. These parents tightly grip their belief that knowledge is power. Overly ambitious parents have to learn the value of experts' experiences, giving deeper meaning to their acquired understanding of giftedness through reading books and researching the Internet. Making the transition to asking for help can be very hard, as these overachieving parents can be consultant shoppers and run to different specialists for answers, which complicates can already complicated problem. Time and patience is required to help these intense families.

THE EFFECTS OF PARENTAL PERCEPTIONS ON THE DEVELOPMENT OF GIFTED POTENTIAL

Giftedness is a legacy that parents hand down to their children. While extreme abilities and talents are remarkable and of the greatest value to humanity, often, these gifts are thwarted by well-meaning but uninformed parents who do not see their blind spots.

Living through Your Child

Deeply embedded ideas about child rearing fueled by unresolved childhood trauma create the often unconscious or conscious need for parents to live through their children. Unfortunately, parental projections lead to rigidly overdetermined reactions and decisions that may actually not be in the child's best interest. From my years of experience consulting with smart parents and my own personal childhood experiences growing up and as a parent of two gifted children, I know that how the parent sees and reacts to his or her bright child is incredibly important to the child's well-being and overall development. Living through your child—giving your child what you did not get in order to feel a sense of wholeness—is a common problem that all parents experience on a conscious or unconscious level. Gifted parents are more intense and tend to overdo their overidentification with their son or daughter with great resolve.

Parental perceptions and reactions, which are based on the parent's personality, values, and life experiences, shape a bright child's future. More often than not, parents want to give to their child what they did not get from their own parents. For example, a new parent who had uninvolved and negligent parents will see their son's or daughter's emotional needs as paramount. I regularly work with mothers and fathers whose lives revolve around their children. While love and attention can be a blessing, it can also make the child overly dependent on their parents' input. With too much attention, children can develop learned helplessness and an unrealistic sense of entitlement, which limit their motivation, internal resources, and confidence.

A telling example of overidentification—living through your children and senseless overdoing—comes Jeanie, who consulted with me about her daughter, Stella. Jeanie grew up basically on her own with only a roof over her head and no positive attention or direction from her parents, who were depressed and unavailable. Jeanie wanted to "give her all" to her daughters, which is totally understandable. But she didn't know when she had done enough. When to stop or to say no eluded her. When I meet her, she was looking for a perfect school for her daughter, a school that would provide a loving community and foster her child's creativity. Jeanie did not want her daughters to be thwarted by conventional limits. She was serious about giving her children choices. Her kids could take any class they wanted. Acquiring toys and clothes was never an issue. Giving to her children what she did not get as a child possessed her. Suffice it to say, I had a lot of work to do to get Jeanie to understand the importance of limiting choices, along with what is reasonable and what is not appropriate. Actually finding real meaning and direction for herself and her family was very difficult for Jeanie because of the emptiness of her childhood. But eventually, Stella and her sister Riley learned to complete their homework. And Jeanie learned that being reasonable and more conventional about her parenting style was valuable.

Another common example of living through one's child involves parents who grew up with serious financial stress and negligence. These parents who as children had too many adult responsibilities are overidentified with their children and seriously give them way too much comfort, luxury, and financial freedom. Indulgence rather than too many unconventional choices limits the child's desire and ability to succeed for himself or herself. Bart is a good example of an overdoer. Bart, unlike Jeanie, knew what he wanted for his children. Bart called me for help in understanding why his sons would not do their homework. A self-made millionaire, he grew up in a home where food was rationed. On days when there was only sour milk in the refrigerator, he went to school hungry. When his mother died of cancer, the family situation became even more stressed and more chaotic. As a child and teenager, Bart had to take care of himself as best he could.

Bart vowed to give his sons a more luxurious childhood than his own. He found success and power in using money to buy things. Unfortunately, Bart took his concerns about his children's comfort too seriously. A chef was employed to make all the meals for the family. Of course, the family home was a mansion that had servants. All kinds of travel experiences, clothes, and toys were provided. Still, Bart's sons had difficulty in private school even with the help of tutors and therapists. What was missing in this family was a sense of reasonableness about what is really necessary. Struggles continually ensued over homework and later drugs. Luxury was not the only thing that these children needed. These entitled boys needed to be treated as normal children with responsibilities. Bart could not grasp the idea that his children needed to learn to be accountable to others. He could not resolve his own childhood suffering through giving too much to his children, but he could not give up trying.

How Conscious Parental Expectations Create Obstacles to Gifted Development

Essentially, a child's destiny is in part founded on the parents' conscious and unconscious visions and expectations for their son or daughter.

The manner in which these expectations are translated and projected is critical to the child's sense of self. Unfortunately, many smart and ambitious parents have serious emotional blind spots that prevent them from being able to see how deeply rooted and unrealistic their hopes for their child can be. Whether parents expect too much or not enough, they can easily distort their perceptions and expectations or be blind to what is in the best interest of their child. What quickly comes to my mind as an example is the parent who wants her child to go to an Ivy League college and does not see the child's genuine artistic nature, need for self-expression, and alternative types of schooling. Or the opposite, the artistic parent who cannot see his child's academic nature and continually insists on creative learning environments.

To intensify and rigidify emotional blindness, parental insights about their own sense of self and how childhood experiences shaped the direction of their life often come from a superficial and judgmental perspective. Other professionals who work with bright children and their parents, such as teachers, administrators, and psychologists, look for easy black and white solutions and understandings. They believe in psychological dynamics that might be found in a fortune cookie. I hear far too many reductionist and vapid remarks from other "experts" that I work with. "The father is not involved; he just works too hard to be a real dad." "The mother had such a chaotic childhood; how can she manage her children?" "The child is being bullied because his parents are too overprotective." "The child is being bullied because of the way his parents fight with one another." There is always more than meets the eye at first glance.

Simplistic formulas—recipes for success—for child rearing become guiding lights for smart parents who should know better. There are no easy answers when you are parenting a spirited child. For example, when I am talking to parents about how they developed their parenting styles, I hear this refrain too often: "My parents were bad or limited in their ability to provide for me. They moved around the country and ignored my education and talents. I will be a better parent than my mother and father. I am striving to be the 'best' parent for my daughter." This typical better-than-my-parents attitude seems to be enough insight for the majority of parents who I work with on a daily basis. (Although I was very motivated to be a different parent than my mother.) Most likely, because mom or dad or both are overidentified with their child, these concerned parents want to give their child what they did not get. In other words, the parents, whether or not they are aware of their motivation, are living through their child. Unfortunately, for many professionals, delving into why parents want to live through their smart kids is just too painful or not worth the time it takes. In my opinion, understanding overidentification with the child is the key to realistically assessing what your child really needs, rather than what you want to give based on the deficits in your childhood.

Understanding what the child's developmental needs are, which are different from what the parent believes the child must have, is crucial to gifted potential and emotional well-being. And yet the difference is ignored for a variety of compelling and time-related reasons. Personally, I am always horrified when I hear the very certain straight and narrow "never enough" narcissistic parenting approach. This unnatural and overly detailed approach justifies the "wanting to do everything right" parenting style. In actuality, raising a bright child from a self-righteous, idealistic, perfectionistic perspective is a recipe for failure. Parents' ambitions and expectations for their son or daughter create and intensify the child's deep need or natural inclination to be doing everything perfectly. Social emotional development will eventually become stalled in a gridlock of self-centeredness between parent and child when thoughts and actions are based on intense perfectionism. Actually, because smart children have the ability to think abstractly, it is natural for them to try to do everything perfectly, which often creates intense anxiety. When parents approach their role with the intention of doing everything perfectly, it can lead to a psychological disaster for the child and the family. When parents believe every little detail is important, a sense of reasonableness and reality is lost. Well-reasoned actions are crucial to parenting effectively.

The Challenges of Gifted Children: Empowering Parents to Maximize Their Child's Potential is based on over 30 years of clinical and consulting experiences with families who seek advice and insight about parenting their spirited children. I will explain in detail why smart parents "overdo" parenting instead of taking a more reasonable approach and just being "good enough." How overparenting affects the very precious and precocious smart child will be outlined. How to approach parenting your bright child with insight, perspective, and knowledge will be presented. Stories and strategies that reflect hands-on experiences of good enough parenting as compared to overdoing parenting or ignoring parenting will be described. These case examples will inspire and enlighten gifted parents about how to get their smart child to do well in school and make friends successfully. As importantly, how parents can stop overdoing every potential crisis and cope with the everyday ups and downs of their spirited child's life will be illustrated.

2

The Smart Parent's Struggle to Be Good Enough

---

*I don' t understand why you would suggest that I be a good enough mother.
I want to be the best and most successful mother.*

—*Crystal*

*When I am upset because I can' t calm Hannah down, I try to decide if I should
follow the Tiger Mom' s advice or the more forgiving approach.*

—*Rozalyn*

ENTANGLEMENTS BETWEEN PARENT AND CHILD DIRECT GIFTED POTENTIAL

It is very likely—almost predictable—that smart parents will have smart kids.
Well, at least that has been my experience of more than 30 years working
with challenging and spirited children and their often frantic, frazzled,
and highly ambitious parents. Studies on heritability—the genetics of
intelligence—predict this connection between parent and child.[1,2] Or more
simply stated, the apple does not fall far from the tree. What is unpredictable
is how smart parents will react to their highly sensitive and dramatically
curious offspring. Unquestionably, parental reactions vary and depend on
what intense parents choose to instill in their spirited children. How the
parents' personalities mesh with the innate temperament of their son or
daughter strongly affects parenting style as well. Of course, the parents'
visions and values are based on their own dreams and expectations. What
parents want to give their children is always very personal. Obviously, there
is no right answer to how concerned parents should react to their bright

child. You are on your own. There is no one book, or books, or experts that can tell you what to do.[3] However, taking a calm and reasonable approach is always a safe way to start.

In my experiences working with spirited families, the development of the child's self-esteem and self-awareness, often referred to as social emotional development, is far more important than an emphasis on achievement and worldly success. Academic, scientific, or artistic genius will develop if a stimulating but nonpressured environment is readily available to the child. Astuteness in a certain realm, talent, or genius will grow and expand if children have self-confidence and a realistic sense of direction that allows them to pursue their giftedness.

Without enough self-awareness and people skills, the most talented child will have difficulty navigating school experiences, and later, their careers, without mom, dad, or a special agent at their side. Learned helplessness will dominate intrinsic motivation and stifle gifted potential. Overly dependent children will need a great deal of tutoring and psychotherapy to move forward on their own. The entanglements and resentments that are bred from too much investment in a child's talents are devastating to both parent and child. In other words, stage mothers and fathers beware. It is far better to let your sons and daughters learn that mistakes are normal learning experiences. Avoid confusing your hopes and expectations with what your child needs or wants in relationship to achievements. Your child's success is not your success.

While parents really need to encourage and help develop their child's intrinsic interests, which will grow into talent, avoiding adult expectations and establishing child-centered goals for emotional, social, academic, and artistic aspects of development is the most crucial and productive parenting agenda. Distinguishing between who you are and who your child may become will keep you from being driven crazy by your child. Without a doubt, engaging your child in decision making is a priceless skill that will serve him or her well into adult life. Smart parents and their children need to learn from their mistakes and to reevaluate their plans. Resilience and the ability to learn through trial and error need to be nurtured through countless hands-on experiences.

To avoid entanglements and resentment from developing, ask yourself:

1. Do I see myself in my child's eyes?
   Good enough reaction: Yes, but I also see my child as unique and special.
   Entangling reaction: Yes, my child is me, but if I focus on my expectations, he will become a better me.
2. Where do my expectations for my child come from?
   Good enough reaction: I am developing visions and hopes from my child's inclinations and interests.

Entangling reaction: I expect my child to follow my lead and listen to my directions.

3. Do my expectations for myself and my child need to be revised?

Good enough reaction: Yes, my expectations will change as my child grows into his own person.

Entangling reaction: No. I want to stick with my original hopes and dreams for my child no matter what.

REACTING TO YOUR CHILD AS GIFTED WITH EXTRA SPECIAL NEEDS

There are a range of reactions that parents have when they sense that their son or daughter may be exceptionally bright. Some parents are delighted and excited, really over the top with anticipation. Positive energy can be helpful. Some parents are totally overwhelmed or confused, often speechless or incredibly sad thinking about the responsibility they have to their son or daughter. Many mothers have shared with me the hours they spent crying when they were informed that their child was gifted. Overwhelmed parents don't think they are smart enough to raise a gifted child. This negative attitude that is tied into poor self-esteem can be crippling to the child and parents alike.

Unfortunately, some parents are in denial about how gifted their child really is and manage to ignore the message that their child needs a different owner's manual. Deniers falsely believe that their son or daughter will be fine no matter what. Actually, this dismissive style of parenting breeds behavioral problems in spirited children. Self-conscious parents experience dread and depression, believing that their son or daughter will suffer in the same way they did fitting in at school academically and socially. These parents believe that their child will be an awkward nerd no matter what they provide. However, they try and do the right thing, which is much better than being negative or in denial.

Convince yourself to find the right owner's manual for your gifted child. Or better yet, write your own manual. Denial, avoidance, dread, and depression will certainly limit your child's potential.[4,5] The more you can understand your child's special challenges and find solutions to his or her learning and emotional issues, the more confident your son or daughter will feel. When smart kids are sure of themselves and well cared for, not spoiled with entitlements, family life will be happier.

EARLY SIGNS OF GIFTEDNESS CAN BE ALARMING WHEN EXPRESSED AS PROBLEMATIC INTENSE NEEDINESS

Whatever parents' reaction to thinking that they have a gifted child, the bright, sensitive, particular child has to be raised and nurtured. Inevitably, parenting problems will arise related to the spirited child's intense sensitiv-ities. The first manifestations of sensitivity and intensity are often seen as "problematic neediness" in the first year of life and continue on and on. Problematic needy behaviors include difficulty being soothed or calmed down by the caregiver and an inordinate amount of separation anxiety from mother. Quite common as well are the child's serious intense interests in certain toys, games, daily rituals, and word play. These intensities are based on interests or fears that normal or average children do not express as dra-matically and loudly. Extremely bright and spirited children can have pas-sions that are alarmingly mature. Temper tantrums can be overwhelming for parents, relatives, and next door neighbors. Separation anxiety from mother can alarm grandparents, babysitters, and teachers. Social anxiety can lead to fear of going to school. Let's look at some examples.

Separation Anxiety

Separation anxiety is a sign of emotional intensity, and it is a source of dis-harmony or tension between mother and infant. The mother or primary caregiver feels frustrated that she cannot calm her infant down. The extent of separation anxiety is much stronger in gifted children than in children who are not gifted and who are less intense. Feelings of loss when separated from the caregiver are profound and difficult to resolve in my experiences with parents and children. The following examples illustrate the extent of this anxiety. While each example is unique and resolved differently, the extent of separation intensity is similar.

Kathy, the youngest of three children, had such serious separation anxiety from her mother Connie from eight months to three years that she had to be held for at least a 30 minutes before settling down to sleep. Letting mom leave her bedroom in the morning to take care of her other sons was an ongoing problem that affected the entire family. Kathy screamed at the top of her lungs when mom started to go downstairs. Connie joined my support group for parents of gifted kids. Gradually over many months of a consistent routine, Kathy learned to self-regulate her anxious feelings related to separa-tion. Kathy' s behavior was a red flag that she was an intense and spirited child who would require her own gifted child parenting manual. Connie learned a great deal from the other mothers in the support group who also had to find solutions to their children's separation anxiety.

Martin was raised with the "attachment parenting" philosophy. He slept in bed with his parents, Joann and Rick, as an infant and toddler. When he was two years old, his parents considered him old enough to have his own bed and bedroom. At first, his parents tried to put him to bed and then let him fall asleep without their presence. However, Marty was a fearful child, and his mother or father had to sit with him every night until he fell asleep.

Marty had a hard time separating from his mother in kindergarten. When he was 5 ½ and in kindergarten, he went back to sleeping with his parents. Finally, Marty's dad, Rick, put his foot down and asked him when he would try to sleep alone. Having to sleep with mom and dad continued until Marty was seven years old. On his seventh birthday, Marty declared he could do it, and he was able to act on his idea that he was old enough to sleep alone. Marty was helped by seeing a child psychologist who encouraged him that he could survive without his mother's presence. Marty's mother, Joann, who was living through her own lack of attention from her mother as a child, needed to be coached into seeing that her son was old enough to separate from her. Joann really struggled with letting go of her fears that her son still needed her.

Daniella had great difficulty sleeping alone. Her parents and their therapist tried every idea known to psychology to get Danny to sleep in her own bed. Even with years of family and individual therapy and medications, Danny could not give up her fear of being alone in her own bedroom when she was at home. Danny did learn to go to sleep away camp and to spend the night with friends and cousins. Her separation anxiety was a serious curiosity to many mental health professionals.

Preston was and still is an intensely imaginative child who is very close to his mother. Preston had issues separating from his mother in preschool. Mom, Rene, had to change preschools several times until she found a school at which Preston felt safe enough to say goodbye to her. This problem separating from mom recurred when Preston started a prestigious and demanding elementary school. Although Preston could say goodbye to his mother when she dropped him off at the big school, he was highly anxious during the school day and had difficulty with children who were bullies. Preston was too anxious to concentrate on learning, and school specialists requested outside tutoring, which just put more pressure on Preston. This additional stress caused this charming child to have panic dreams about going to school. Anxiety and missing mom were curtailed when the family chose a new school that had a more creative approach to learning and was closer to home. Separation anxiety was a theme is this child's emotional life.

Passionate Interests

Passionate interests are a sign of intellectual curiosity, emotional intensity, and the drive to focus and concentrate. Passionate interests make transitions very difficult for gifted children. Here are some examples of early passions.

Steven started to identify letters at the age of 11 months. He continued to look through books and by 15 months, he was reading short words and memorizing the text in his story books. Steven's interest in reading continued, and by age three, he was a fluent reader. In contrast, Steven refused to learn to draw until he was instructed in kindergarten. Steven transferred his interest in reading to learning all about Star Wars characters, which he could not seem to stop talking about when he entered kindergarten. Changing Steven's focus from his own interests was always difficult.

Emily started putting puzzles together at one year of age. She could not stop making puzzles because it was the only activity that seemed to calm her down. Her parents kept finding more and more complicated puzzles for their daughter to complete. While upgraded puzzles was a soothing activity, social skills were not given enough attention. Helping Emily develop social skills was a very serious problem that took many years to solve and included many different types of school experiences.

Ronald's his love of dinosaurs started early in his second year of life. Parents, grandparents, aunts, and uncles gave him toy dinosaurs from all kinds of stores, both local and in faraway lands. Ron had a huge collection. He memorized all of their long names. Later, by age three, he had learned to read their names. Understandably, Ronnie was bored at school with the learning of the traditional ABCs. His mother sought out advice on how to keep Ron engaged at school. When Ron was stressed by family issues or bullying at school, he would retreat into his own interests and not pay attention at school.

Miranda had three older cousins who gave her their collection of "hand me downs." Miranda loved trying on different outfits, and by age two, she was very particular about what she wanted to wear. She would change her clothes three or four times a day and drive her mother and sisters "batty." Setting limits for clothes changes was challenging for the entire family because Miranda was so interested in her imaginational intensity, which took the form of fashion. Gradually, Miranda learned that she could not spend as much time as she wanted to getting ready for school.

Social Issues

Finding friends for gifted children can be extremely challenging, as bright kids seem to prefer other smart kids, adults, or older children. Here are some examples of common social difficulties.

Susan was a high-strung baby and was very particular about what she played with as an infant and toddler. Her mother found that Susan loved dolls, and she was calm and content playing with her collection. Dolls became an easy answer to keeping this curious child happy and easy to deal with in most situations. Unfortunately, when Susan started preschool, she did not have enough of the social skills necessary to interact with other children. Preschool teachers were alarmed and suggested that Susan be screened for autistic spectrum disorder. Mom had to look for a parent support group and other advice to help broaden her daughter's range of social activities. As mom learned from other moms with gifted kids how to set limits, she felt less inclined to think that she would go crazy with Susan. And Susan learned some important social skills about making friends. Today, Susan is known as the cool gifted kid in fourth grade.

Scarlet was a shy child who managed to fit in socially at a small Montessori school. When she started kindergarten at a neighborhood public school, Scarlet was very overwhelmed by the extra children in her class, and she often wandered around the classroom. Her teacher decided to let Scarlett read in the corner when she was distracted by too much noise. This intervention was very helpful to Scarlet's progress in kindergarten. Gradually, Scarlett learned to interact with her classmates, which took a lot of parental and teacher conviction along with time and patience.

Brandon was an only child who was the center of his parents' attention. He did not attend Mommy and Me classes or preschool because he would throw temper tantrums and hit other children. In kindergarten, he had a very difficult time adjusting to the class rules. An Individualized Education Plan (IEP) was used to provide Brandon with special attention from the resource specialists. But behavioral interventions only seemed to make Brandon's anger problems more serious. Brandon felt that he was being criticized by the interventions, which made him feel humiliated. When mom enrolled her son in a small Montessori school that allowed for individual development and found a therapist to help Brandon self-regulate his intense feelings, he was able to develop the social skills he needed for school. His mom and dad attended parenting groups, which helped them understand their son's sometimes un-understandable behavior.

COPING WITH EARLY PROBLEMATIC INTENSITY AND NEEDINESS

Parents react to their child's idiosyncratic or "weird" behavior just as intensely as their spirited children do. They are always wondering what they should do, as if there were one right way to handle their child's emotional intensity. It would be helpful if really smart "go-getter" parents understood that a calm good enough reaction to their son's or daughter's demands is better than an intense perfectionist reaction. In other words, your child does not have to collect every single dinosaur known to humans, be encouraged to understand his or her deepest fears from an adult perspective, or be happy and engaged all of the time with an activity such as putting puzzles together. Good enough parenting reactions—validation and reasonableness—are actually the emotionally healthy way to react to your child's emotions and interests. And they are enough.

Showing your son or daughter that you are attuned to their varying states of mind and that you can validate their feelings is critical. Being able to tolerate your son's or daughter's excitement, curiosity, anger, and frustration is essential to their positive sense of self. In contrast, holding onto each of your child's intense feelings or demands as if it were a sign of long-range emotional health or talent development is literally crazy making for both parent and child.[6] Perfectionist parenting is an intense form of overdoing attentiveness that is sure to make you feel overwhelmed and unsure of yourself. Reacting, but not overreacting, to your child's feelings helps him or her develop a sense of inner resources and helps them self-regulate and calm down. Your calmness lets your child see and experience you as a separate person. Reacting as a good enough parent should be your first and foremost goal if you have a bright and intensely spirited children. Unfortunately, understanding the meaning of good enough is very difficult for smart parents because it is counterintuitive to their general driven perfectionist approach to life.

Parents who attend my parenting group shared some thoughts about trying to be less intense and less perfectionist.

Randy: *I worry my daughter Julie feels abandoned and that I have broken her trust. I worry that I am too cold and scarring her. I worry that I am misparenting her. The reality is that Julia is angry that I won't hold her because she has come to expect it.*

Rita: *When Monica cries, I feel like a bad mother and that I am creating a permanent scar in her heart that she will hold against me when she is older. What is really happening is that Monica is trying to get my attention, and in another moment, she will forget what she was crying about in the first place.*

Rene: *It is important to not overthink everything. Sometimes Ted is just tired and does not want to play with his friends. I start to believe that he will be awkward socially, which is just me making everyday occurrences more meaningful and bigger than they need to be.*

What is most apparent from working with parents of gifted kids is the reality that the more you give, the more they will take. You have to be careful not to overdo or overthink the issues your child is struggling with. Try to be practical and realistic, as this attitude will calm the situation down. When a situation is calmer, it is easier to find a solution.

GOOD ENOUGH PARENTING STYLE MOST EFFECTIVE WITH GIFTED KIDS

Good enough parenting is based on the psychological theories of Donald Winnicott, a British psychoanalyst who wrote about attachment issues between parent and growing child. Specifically, Winnicott was interested in how parents and children separate from one another in a healthy and adaptive way. Winnicott believed that parent-child attachment is based on a love between two imperfect individuals—parent and infant. The good enough parent is attentive to the child's emotional and physical needs without believing narcissistically that he or she is a perfect parent and the child is perfect as well. The good enough parent sees the importance of reliability and consistency, which allows the child to feel comfortable with dependency and with separation. The good enough parent can validate and tolerate his or her son's or daughter's intense feelings without giving into unreasonable demands.[7]

Good enough parents respond to their growing child's physical and emotional needs based on their sense of their child. In other words, they know from their early parenting of the child if he or she is high strung, more mild mannered, or somewhere in between. Because infants and toddlers cannot explain their thoughts and feelings, parents have to try to understand what might be going on in their children's lives based on their knowledge of the children's previous reactions. Emotional and cognitive connection through attunement and understanding of the child's experience is the challenge of good enough parenting. In addition, parents have to have a vision for their children's long-range well-being. Understanding that optimal frustration is a very important part of affective attunement to the growing child is essential. In other words, the parent may know that the child is angry and validate his or her feeling without allowing the child to act out his or her anger through disruptive behavior. For example, you can say, "I know you are angry with your sister, but I can't let you hit her" or, "I know you want to tear up your homework because you think it is not good enough. Please listen to me; your paper is fine."

It sounds obvious, and somewhat simpleminded, but of course, the child and parent are not one. They are two separate individuals, even though the parent naturally sees himself of herself in the child's eyes, which creates confusion and overidentification between parent and child. The parent is not the child's best friend, twin, or expensive toy. The roles and needs of both parents and children are distinctive and important. While your son or daughter cannot explain his or her need for your reliability and maturity, the child clearly needs the stability of the your long-range vision about life. The child needs a parent he or she can trust to reflect on his or her actions and attempt to bridge misunderstandings when they occur. When parents take the upper hand and try to resolve misunderstandings fairly, the bond or attachment between parent and child is strengthened. Natural mistakes are inevitable and provide for optimal frustrations, which teach the child and parent resilience.

In my experiences working with gifted parents of gifted children, it is rare to speak to a parent who emotionally understands the concept of good enough. In fact, usually the parents' reaction is to be put off by this well-documented concept because they are looking for the competitive edge that will help them be the best parents they can be. Concerned parents naturally want their kids to be successful and better prepared for life than they have been. Unfortunately, far too often, parents are blindsided to the dark side of their pressured and perfectionist outlook. Overwrought children can become depressed or develop antisocial behaviors. Drug use, sexual acting out, school delinquency, and even suicide attempts are common in gifted teenagers who have lived with too many challenges from schools and parents. Your overdetermined and extravagant expectations for your son or daughter can ultimately make you feel out of control and negative about who you are as a parent. When you feel out of control, your child can make you feel crazy!

Ask yourself:

1. Will it be hard for me to raise a gifted child?

    Good enough reaction: Yes, I am sure that there will be ups and downs as my child grows.

    Entangled reaction: No, I can do perfectly whatever I set my mind to do. I have the time and money to pursue whatever help my child may need.

2. How is my child different from me?

    Good enough reaction: Well, I am sure that my son has some of his father's qualities and some of my qualities. I am going to work on helping him be an individual in his own right.

    Entangled reaction: I want my son to be just like me when he grows up.

3. What lessons did I learn from my family that are worth following?

    Good enough reaction: My family believed in the importance of love and education. Otherwise, they were way too isolated from other families.

    Entangled reaction: I will do the complete opposite of whatever my family believed in. I will be better than they are because I know where they made their mistakes.

4. How can I help myself stop overthinking what I should do when my child is unhappy?

    Good enough reaction: I can talk to other parents with children who are the same age and read about possible solutions.[8]

    Entangled reaction: I will never let my child cry or be unhappy. I don't want her to suffer in the same way that I suffered.

PERFECT PARENTING: ENTITLEMENT AND INTENSITY IN GIFTED CHILDREN

Without a doubt, having a smart parent can contribute enormously to a precocious child's growth and development. Parents with success in their back pocket tend to try harder and use their resources very effectively to resolve issues related to overexcitabilities, emotional intensity, schooling, child care, and all of the extras. Thoughtful parents are very capable of draw-ing up complicated plans and strategies to provide for their growing kids in so many creative ways. Thinking about how to manage their son's or daughter's intellectual and emotional well-being is important and compel-ling. The need to provide experiences with sports, art classes, and travel makes their list of concerns. Play dates are now considered a "must do" for parents concerned with raising a well-adjusted youngster.

Still, parenthood is stressful for very bright people. In fact, extremely bright parents face raising children with a great deal of trepidation. They are extremely intense about being successful and tend to see parenting success in black and white—good or bad. Often, they confuse the process of raising a well-adjusted child with the process of achieving career or finan-cial success. Thinking, and then believing, that there is one right or certain path to follow, concerned parents are often confused or overwhelmed by small situations that seem larger than life when they don't work out as planned. For example, Judy forgetting to hand in her homework or Tom bit-ing Harry at preschool can be blown up into major events rather than just being seen as part of the life of a child.

Parents who have "made it" in life because they are hardworking, are persistent, and value being "know it alls" can be clueless about what to really look for in their child's behavior. Being a "know it all" can make you feel very out of control when your child is out of synch with your reasonable demands for his or her behavior. I am including here those overachieving parents who have read a lot of books and blogs about how to parent. Admittedly, they have a lot of knowledge about what to expect. Moms and dads need to learn that knowledge is not equivalent to experience with one's own child when it comes to parenting. Trial and error is the best way to develop parenting strategies. There are no pat answers for raising a spirited child.

Highly motivated, driven parents tend to measure career success and parenting with the same yardstick. This is a huge mistake. Clearly, career success and parenting success are very different parts of life's experiences and need to be seen from different perspectives. This simple idea may be easy to understand intellectually but very hard to process with emotional clarity. Parents may know that being nurturing, consistent, and decisive with their children is important and very difficult to measure objectively. And yet, they are quick to make serious harsh positive or negative proclamations about their effectiveness as parents when they are struggling with getting homework completed or a social skills issue.

Gifted parents are very sensitive, have issues with insecurity, and tend to believe that they have to be perfect almost every moment of their lives. They resolve to be the best parents they can be. Unfortunately, sometimes they don't even have a clue about how to proceed and subsequently "overdo," intel-lectualize, or are too rigid when making decisions about feeding, sleeping, play dates and school placement. Overdoing only makes these issues more intense, crazy making, and confusing for both parent and child.

Some of the mothers in my parenting group shed light on this very issue of insecurity, confusion, and their mission to do a perfect job of parenting.

Validation of My Stress Is Useful

Jeanette: *Some days are so hard. Sam is angry with me and in trouble at school. I go through all of my parenting books and talk with my sister-in-law, but I can't calm down. Finally, I start reading blogs on the Internet. I find a mom who has a son with my son's problems. I feel validated and not so alone and confused. When someone understands how hard it is to raise a gifted child, my job of raising him is more manageable.*

Rene: *Participating in the parenting group for raising gifted kids has been invaluable. I have achieved a new level of acceptance and understanding of my child's differences. Hearing the stories of other parents with similar challenges has normalized behaviors that I perceived as extreme. Establishing a sense of the norm for gifted kids helped alleviate some of my isolation and confusion. My fears are alleviated in group by other mothers. I feel validated that my struggles are real.*

Seeking Out the Truth

Mia: *I have read every good book on parenting. I have belonged to several Mommy and Me groups. My husband and his parents are supportive of my decisions. I am a highly educated and successful professional woman. I wish that I could find the answer to being the best parent I can be. When Grace has a meltdown, I am totally lost. Finding support from other people who understand and are not critical of me is helpful.*

Isabelle: *I am not sure what to do about my daughter Katie's school. She is very shy, and the head of the French school says that she is not making friends. My husband wants Katie to be bilingual because he had to give up his language when he came to the United States. Madam Lorene says Katie needs a different kind of school. I wish that I could find the right answer to what school is best for Katie.*

Not Making My Mother's Mistakes

Darcy: *I thought my husband and I were doing everything right. I didn't want to be indifferent like my mother, who was never there for me when my father abused me. Maybe I have done too much. Is Spencer too entitled or just a know it all? I hope next year he will get along better with his teachers and classmates. I wonder why I am taking this situation so personally.*

Deannie: *My mother was only 16 when she had me. She never paid attention to me. I don't think she was prepared to be my mother. I have struggled to not make my mother's mistakes. I wonder, did I go too far? Is Tanya too sure of herself? What can I do to help her listen to reasonable ideas?*

Ask yourself:

1. Can I list five ways that being a parent is a new kind of experience for me?
2. How will I know that I am doing a good job as a parent? What criteria will point to my success?
3. How can I develop confidence in my parenting skills?

BEWARE: FAMILY AND CLOSE FRIENDS CAN UNDERMINE PARENTAL CONFIDENCE

Grandma and grandpa or other friends and relatives who think that they are capable of giving older-and-better advice show concern about your high-strung, energetic, developing infant, toddler, school-age child, or teenager. *Actually*, in reality, well-meaning outsiders can make parents feel inadequate. Who you listen to for feedback and support is critical. Having your spouse on the same page with you when you are making decisions is one right thing to do. Finding parents who have similar problems is also essential. Let's look at some examples of parents struggling to develop confidence in their parental roles.

The Unprepared Parents: An Old-Fashioned Problem?

Not having time to review all of your options in child rearing is more common than you think. Not every new parent has a library on child development or has made an advanced choice about pregnancy, even in today's world of instant information access and health planning.

Ann is a young mother who is *not* up to date on the latest child rearing literature. Ann's pregnancy was unplanned. But still, having a baby is a life-changing decision that Ann definitely takes very seriously with James, her husband. James is still in medical school, and he leaves the really serious decisions about how to raise their son to his wife. James is pressured by the enormous amount of studying he must do to keep up with his class. Without any knowledge or hands-on experiences with children, Ann turns to her mother and her husband's Grandma Lyn for advice and support. Neither set of grandparents is prepared for baby Robert. They are all in shock. Ann is so young to be taking on motherhood. All of the grandparents had hoped that Ann would have a career before having children. Her mother, Sarah, is tentative about making an emotional connection with her daughter at this point in her life and her new grandson. Sarah continues to wish that things were different.

On dad's side of the family, Grandma Lyn is very outspoken and starts speaking critically of Ann's approach almost at once. Grandma Lyn thinks that her brand new grandbaby Robert is just "too fussy" and needs too much attention. Lyn wants Robert on a strict feeding and sleeping schedule. As might be expected, Robert is hungry when he is hungry, which makes it hard for Ann to be as rigid as his grandmother suggests. Keeping to a feeding and sleeping schedule is frustrating. Ann's mother, Sarah, continues to be of no help. Ann has to look around—or rather, search high and low—to find a pediatrician who can understand and react to all of her concerns with her firstborn son. While overwhelmed, Ann is determined to get the best care for herself and her son. After many tries, Ann finds a pediatrician who can understand and not judge her "perceived difficulties" being a parent to Robert. Ann finds a parent support group at her son's Mommy and Me class, which is very helpful because she comes to see that other mothers have similar problems with their children.

Ann gradually learns to follows her intuition about people who can help her. Ann takes charge of decision making because she *is* in charge and is good at working out what is best for their small family. Dad, who is always busy with school, manages to be a playful friend to his child, which helps. Grandma Lyn is not happy about how her grandson is being cared for. She has the same sort of complaints about her granddaughter Elli when she is born three years later. Elli always wants to be held. Elli is very particular about who feeds and changes her. Grandma Sarah remains in the background, indifferent to her daughter's need for validation. By now, Ann is not listening to the grandparents' advice, which is an enormous step forward. But Ann still feels like she might be making a lot of mistakes. Grandparent pressure coupled with grandparent disinterest has created a sense of insecurity for this young family.

Learning from Ann and James's Experiences

Clearly, Ann's heart is in the right place, but her lack of knowledge and preparation for having a child have created uncertainty and confusion about how to be a good enough mother. Understandably, Ann looks to her parents and her husband's parents for help. Unfortunately, Robert and Elli's grandparents are too rigid and too emotionally limited to provide any meaningful support. They are able to provide short sessions of child care and financial assistance, which makes life easier and more manageable. However, they are very negligent about providing positive energy. Searching for a pediatrician who can deal with Ann's intense anxiety is a good move because it teaches Ann to trust her intuition about people who can help her. Ann learns that she is the primary parent in charge of her children's well-being. Ann gains confidence in her choices and builds more confidence in herself as the years go by. While Ann's husband James does no contribute his share to the parental unit decision making, he is present and has good caregiving instincts. Grandparent support is focused on extras for the children.

The Well Prepared: "Parents of the Internet Generation"

Supposedly well-prepared parents think that all information on child development is only a second away on the Internet. Another part of their faulty thinking includes believing that their money can lead them to find the perfect help.

Crystal, a well-known plastic surgeon, is very up to date on what to expect when one is expecting. She is in her mid-30s and used fertility treatments to get pregnant. Crystal has read a lot of parenting books and has discussed the arrival of her daughter at length with her husband and their medical colleagues. Unlike Ann, she believes she is prepared for her role as a mother. In fact, Dr. Crystal is very sure of herself because she is so successful in her medical career. Crystal knows how to be in charge and how to give orders. All of the grandparents seem to rely on and support her judgment in most matters related to child rearing.

When Crystal gives birth to her daughter, she immediately takes charge of decision making. Stuart, her husband, is very nonassertive regarding parenting. He is either indifferent or feels extremely burdened by his baby daughter, Isabella. Stuart tries to rationalize that grandparent support—which is generous, with extravagant gifts and flexible availability for child care—makes up for his emotional absence. All feedback to Crystal about Isabella is given in easy to hear words. No one in the family dares to be critical of mom, let alone make suggestions. In reality, Crystal is in serious need of some real hands emotional insight to deal with her daughter.

Unexpectedly, Isabella is a hard to handle child. She is fussy and has difficulty settling down for a nap. Once she is finally put to sleep in her crib, Isabella needs very little sleep compared to other infants her mother has encountered. As she grows into toddlerhood, Isabella has a hard time listening to her mother. Crystal takes her to the pediatrician to have her hearing checked. Predictably, Isabella's hearing is fine. She just does not want to listen to her mom. Even though Crystal has found the "best" pediatrician in her community, she often feels frustrated that Dr. Jill is so cold and objective when giving directions on how to deal with little Isabella. Crystal struggles hard to stay calm. She does not panic about her ability to be a mom. When she has had a frustrating day at her office and then after work with her long-awaited daughter, Crystal feels totally discouraged and at her wits end. She believes that no one understands what she is going through. All Crystal's advisors seem to give remote suggestions as they try to decide if Isabella fits into a *Diagnostic and Statistical Manual of Mental Disorders IV*, revised

(DSM-IV-R) category. They prescribe possible solutions to Isabel' sleeping problems. A more caring approach that looks at Crystal' anxiety about being a mother is not considered.

Because Stuart is of no help with Isabella, a morning nanny and an evening nanny are employed to help with the little girl. Crystal suffers from postpartum depression and seeks help from a mental health professional, Dr. Maloney, who prescribes antidepressants. These medications alleviate some of her crying symptoms and desire to stay in bed. Overall, expert help has managed some of the family's problems. Professional help has also served to alienate this overachieving, "let's get it done" working mother. Eventually, Crystal finds a parenting group with whom she can share her concerns about Isabella. Finding help from other mothers is something that becomes a strategy for Crystal when she feels uncertain about what is her best option for Isabella.

Learning from Crystal's and Stuart's Experiences

Crystal is highly prepared on a pragmatic level to care for her daughter. But unresolved personal issues centered on perfectionism are brought up by motherhood, which makes Crystal feel very vulnerable, uncertain, and yes, crazy. Crystal can't be the perfect mother. She does not know where to turn for "real" help. Friends and grandparents are reluctant or too intimidated to make suggestions. When concerned relatives and friends do offer advice, Crystal reacts strongly, as she does not like to feel like she is making a mistake. Crystal learns that she can get help from other parents in her community. Most importantly, Crystal begins to understand that she can learn how to be a mom through trial and error. As her child grows, Crystal learns to work as a member of a team without being the leader. Crystal learns that she does not always have to perform her role as mother flawlessly. Accepting that she can not be a perfect mother is extremely difficult for Crystal.

The Overwhelmed Parents: "Never Enough Thinkers and Doers"

Wanting to do and give everything to their son or daughter torments the lives of these parents, whose childhoods were emotionally empty of nurturing and love. Parental emotional abandonment has left obvious scars on their sense of self. Without reliable role models parenting is very difficult for them. Setting limits can seem impossible.

Kayla and Jonah are self-made successes in Hollywood. All of their dear friends have children. Their friends seem quite capable of managing their children's everyday life. Kayla and Jonah agree that having a family will make their lives more meaningful. Both come from very different, but highly dysfunctional, families. Relying on relatives seems like an unlikely option when it comes to childcare questions or emotional support. Kayla gets pregnant easily even though she is older. Her pregnancy is difficult, and Jonah is working out of town at the end of her pregnancy. Daniella, their daughter, is a sensitive and demanding infant. Jonah is shocked by the feelings of responsibility that he has in his role as a dad. In contrast, Kayla is so delighted. She loves being a mother, even though she is not sure what it really means to be a mother.

Kayla, who can't even have a conversation with her parents, has never had any experience with children and feels lost when she can't comfort her daughter. Fortunately, there is enough help in the house, and Kayla does not have to go back to work. Daniella is like an Energizer bunny who needs constant attention and stimulation. Kayla establishes an organic parenting style that tries to take into account all of the latest parenting techniques. Mother and daughter are continually involved in one activity or another. Kayla and Jonah take their attempts to give what they did not get too far. For example, Kayla keeps 10 different flavors of ice cream in her freezer so that Danny can make a choice. Kayla really does not know when she has done enough for Daniella.

Jonah works long hours and is tired when he comes home. He wishes that his once efficient wife could just figure out how to calm their daughter down. Jonah believes that he can outsource the crying and sleeping problem to an expert and then Kayla will be able to have dinner on the table when he leaves the set. His buddies on set suggest that they hire the "sleep fairies" to come over and put Danny to sleep. This idea is as ridiculous as it sounds. Jonah learns the hard way that life with Daniella evolves very differently than life on the family sitcoms he writes and produces.

The fantasy of finding the one right expert to calm Daniella down is never realized. Life never goes back to the prechildren days. Kayla and Jonah are smart enough and persistent enough to eventually understand that they are on their own and have to find people to help them with their parenting problems. Because they are members of a religious community, they turn to religious leaders and teachers for guidance. Still, Kayla feels like something is missing in her parenting approach. She feels unsure of herself as a mother because setting limits for her daughter makes her feel "mean" and also makes Danny more clingy and intense. It is rare for Kayla to believe she has done enough, even with all of her resources. Still, she tackles each day with fervor, knowing that she is a better mother than her own mother was. Jonah just tries to keep up with his wife and child while he pursues his successful career.

Learning from Kayla's and Jonah's Experiences

Kayla loves motherhood even though her daughter is very intense, and it is hard to settle Danny down and contain her intensity. Kayla can accept and revel in the reality that having a child has changed her life for the best. Jonah has a harder time dealing with parenthood and often panics that he is not doing enough. He follows Kayla's lead and is extremely loving and kind with his daughter. Both parents have to develop and hold onto expectations for their child. They can become so concerned about giving what they did not get to their daughter that they forget to set limits. Drawing the line between child needs and parental decisions is a serious challenge. Although Kayla may feel like she is an older mother and not totally in sync with the younger moms, she works very hard to make decisions that are in the family's best interests. She really outshines the younger moms because she is so intent. Learning to ask for help is hard for Kayla, even though her husband is so encouraging. Eventually Kayla, who grew up on her own, learns that other people can and will help her. The couple's deep acceptance of one another through all of the trials and tribulations of raising a gifted daughter pays off for this family.

The parents described in this chapter all have had to deal with outside forces of family, friends, and social networks that surround their family structure. They have all survived the steep learning curves related to listening to the advice of others when they became parents. Ann learns to find true supports to help with her concerns regarding her children. Crystal learns that she cannot be the perfect mother, and she pursues being a good enough mother. Kayla learns that asking for help in saying "no" is very useful. Learning to deal with being a parent is directly related to learning to get along with other people whose role in your life is not established by professional boundaries or even friendship boundaries. Developing confidence in your decisions as a parent is also directly related to your relationship with the community that your family chooses to engage with directly.

Eventually, the born to succeed parent will definitely get direct or indirect messages that their son or daughter is not "normal." Messages about mom's and dad's inability to provide structure for their gifted child are always clearly communicated. Already, smart parents are learning that their gifted child needs a different parent's manual from the next door neighbor's child, who is calm and easier to put to sleep and take on day trips. It is true that gifted parents who seek out the "owners' manual" for gifted kids will optimize their emotional and financial resources.

Ask yourself:

Who can I turn to when I need support and validation for my parenting?
Does my husband, wife, or partner help with decision making?
Am I trying to balance too much by working full time?
Do I need something else in my life besides my child?

CONCLUSIONS

Be Realistic about What Your Child Needs and What You Can Give

Actually, not all gifted parents are perfectionists. But the parents who seek out help and advice from teachers and experts on gifted children have a tendency to want to do everything right. Gifted parents are predictably intense and sensitive because of their drive to be the best they can be. They see and identify with the unique issues of their smart child. Some parents will talk about their concerns, and other parents will just keep those concerns buried deep inside of themselves. Inevitably, parents will have to react to their own concerns because they will be amplified by their social network of family, school, and friends. Depending on their own emotional resources, perfectionism can be helpful or self-destructive. In other words, trying to do your best within reasonable limits is very useful in some situations. However, always having to be the best at everything sends the message to your child that perfectionism is very important. When you give your child the message to be a perfectionist, you are driving off the cliff and into disaster.

Parents who have insight into their own motivation for developing a way to relate to their child will have fewer overwhelming moments. Unrealistic expectations or living through your child will confuse and undermine your decision making and authority. Try to evaluate how serious a problem is in relationship to your child. Some problems are small. Some issues are more serious. Getting a handle on what will work and what will make your life less stressful is extremely important. Think about the world around your family. Let it in, but don't put outsiders on your board of directors. Have a policy about making mistakes and value your mistakes.

Strategies for Being a Good Enough Parent

1. Try to develop your real authentic self-confidence as a parent based on knowledge and experience.
2. Learn that making mistakes is inevitable and that rethinking plans will optimize your child's healthy development.
3. Model mistake-making behavior so that your son or daughter learns from you how to make mistakes and continue on with a project.
4. Don't spend time wishing your child were different and easier to handle.
5. Don't rely on grandparents, friends, teachers, or other experts who are critical of you because they just don't understand. Rather, find people who understand you and validate your point of view.
6. Don't long for a really calm, normal home life, as you will just feel frustrated and miss the really special aspects of your child growing up.
7. Enjoy the rocky road of parenthood when you can.

8. Get used to your child's argumentative, intense nature and try to keep both of you under control, as you will both feel less overwhelmed and hopeless.
9. Remember, you are a gardener who has to know when your child needs water and when he or she has had enough.
10. Find people in your life that embrace your journey and spend as much time as you can developing their friendships.

3

Discipline and Setting Limits for Gifted Children Is Challenging

It can be difficult to effectively set limits because my daughters are very persistent and do not back down easily when they want something. Often, when I am enforcing a limit, I have to endure a lengthy period of time negotiating, insisting, and possibly an all-out meltdown. Intense reactions also make setting limits difficult. Dealing with meltdowns and tantrums is exhausting and can take up a lot of time, making the original act of enforcing a limit almost seems less important. I think it becomes very important to figure out which limits really matter and let go of some of the small stuff simply to avoid a life of constant battles. Finding balance is always key.

—Leslie

WHY IS IT SO HARD TO DRAW THE LINE BETWEEN WHAT IS ACCEPTABLE AND WHAT IS OFF LIMITS?

Establishing clear emotional boundaries between parent and child can be tricky and very difficult. Consider the following little story, which I call "Who Is the Parent?"

Frank, a devoted dad, arrives home after a long day at work. His wife Jenny and son Michael are engaged in an intense discussion. "Why are you two upset with each other?" he asks calmly.

Jenny explains that Michael won't stop building another one of his Lego spaceships. "His stubbornness is frustrating to me," she adds.

Michael bitterly complains that his homework is boring and is "only for stupid kids!"

Harry, their two-year-old son, is fussy because Michael woke him early from his nap to play Batman and Superman. Now, Harry wants candy instead of a healthy dinner. Jenny doesn't give in, and Harry doesn't stop asking. Well, really he demands *candy in a manner that stopped being cute six months ago.*

Frank silently wonders why he and Jenny decided to have children.

"Who is the parent here?" he whispers to Jenny. "The kids are running the house. Why won't Harry and Michael listen to you?"

Getting gifted kids to listen to you and accept boundaries of acceptable behavior is the parents' basic and primary challenge. And let me underline the point that the explanation for this challenge cannot be found in the latest parenting book on discipline in 10 easy steps. Rather, the explanation lies in understanding that setting limits is a complicated phenomenon, a subjective process related to the closeness of the parent-child attachment. Like a mirror, parents see parts of themselves in their child's eyes.[1] Psychologists and psychiatrists call this phenomenon of seeing oneself in others projection. From certain details in an interpersonal interaction, a mother involved with caretaking sees her child crying and recalls her own pain of feeling unattended to in her childhood. The mother, as she experiences her own frightening memories, sees them as if they are real in her child. The feelings of mother and child get confused.[2]

Here is another interesting example. Recently, my identical twin sister Marjorie telephoned me to say that she was sending a picture of her 11-month-old granddaughter, who she tells me "looks just like you when you were a baby." Marjorie is making part of a memory fragment real in identifying me with her granddaughter. Unfortunately, in our twin baby pictures, no one can tell Marjorie and me apart! Why does Marjorie not see herself, just me—her twin sister? I guess it's one of those hard to explain twin things and an excellent example of projective identification. In other words, you see what your mind and heart are programmed to see and focus on this aspect of a relationship.

Another example from a slightly different positive perspective involves the mother who was treated by her family as the ugly duckling. This mother fears the humiliation of being unattractive for her daughter and focuses on the beauty in her daughter's face. The parent's positive vision for her child is a form of projective identification with the child, and it provides reparenting for the parents. Reparenting occurs when you give your child what you lacked as a child and desperately wanted. You reparent yourself by giving to your child what you didn't get. You enjoy your gift of attentiveness through your child's eyes. Seeing parts of yourself in your child's eyes can make setting limits difficult and confusing.[3]

SETTING LIMITS: ATTACHMENT ISSUES MAKE SAYING NO PAINFUL AND CONFUSING

Attachment between parent and infant is based on an almost magical and compelling chemistry. Connecting with your infant as an evolving parent involves subjective or personal decisions that are based on your sense of the world and your identity. Simply stated, your personality connects with your infant's genetic personality endowment, which we refer to as temperament. For example, a timid mother with a fussy baby will see her child as helpless and in need of a great deal of attention. A more confident mom with a fussy baby will be less apprehensive about her child's well-being and perhaps less anxious about how much attention to give. The child will be less demanding because the mother will be less sensitive to the child's demands. The permutations of the caregiver's personality and the child's innate personality go on and on. There is always an interactive mixture between the child's temperament and the parent's personality and life experiences.[4]

Parental identification with the infant is normal and healthy to a point. But it is especially important for parents to be aware of their projections and identifications so that these mindsets don't get out of control and become too powerful. Projection can take over practical and actual reality. A mother who feels helpless and is depressed will project her helpless feelings onto her son or daughter. The infant can become lethargic or overly energetic and act out the mother's negativity. The young child's behaviors, based to some extent on projection and identification, can become self-fulfilling prophecies that wrongly direct the child. When half-truths become real, powerful false self-adaptations retard or invade the development of the "true self." The child takes on the mother's or father's self-destructive identity.[5] For example, the impulsive parent models impulsive behavior that the child acts out and takes on as part of his or her identity. Or the child withdraws to give parents the space they think they need to be content.

As mothers and fathers live and relive their own lives through their attachment to their child, conflicts over discipline begin to develop, which creates disharmony between parent and child. Setting limits can get emotionally confusing for the parent. And the know-it-all gifted kid can get the upper hand in the conflict. On a psychological level, the smart and intuitive child becomes the parent or the parentified child, barking out orders to his or her parents that are unsafe and inappropriate. For example, parents want their child to be content all of the time and so never say "no." When in a crisis, the parents have to say "no," and the extremely intense and spirited child will not listen. Unfortunately, often the parentified child has never learned to listen. What is missing in a crisis situation is the reality that mom and dad are in charge.

Confusion over setting limits gives the gifted child too much power over his or her parents, and consequences can become an ongoing negotiation. Children need to develop their own sense of consequences to gradually separate from their parents and develop individuality. For example, curiosity may be more important to a child then contentment. Parents in their zealous endorsement of contentment are blind to the child's interest in exploration. Simply stated, for personality development to be nonconflicted, it has to be based on the child's sensibility, not the parents' visions, expectations, and values. The gifted child most likely values satisfying his or her intensity, while the parent may just long for a sense of calm and peace. No one in the family is satisfied by confusion over appropriate limits.

I realize that the idea of seeing yourself in your child's eyes is very abstract. To make it more real and alive, I am sharing what some of the parents in my weekly support group for families with gifted children had to say about the closeness, or the sense of oneness, they felt with their infants and children. These reflections will give you a sense of what I mean about projection and identification between parent and child—how parents sees themselves in their child or through their child. In each example, parents react by giving the child what they wanted for themselves as children.

Leslie grew up in a loving but disadvantaged family that had no particular educational savvy about raising children. She consciously longed for more her mother to pay special attention to her strengths, but her own mother left her to figure out life on her own. Leslie shares her thoughts about the oneness, or the early attachment, she had with her daughter Emily Jean, which reveal her own longings to be special:

> I didn't know that I was going to feel that connected to Emily Jean. From the get-go, her nature demanded a great deal of closeness. I sang to her. I danced with her. I walked with her in a baby sling. All of this closeness made me feel very attached to her.

Leslie's experience as a new mother demonstrates the power of identification between mother and child. Leslie sees her own unmet needs in her child's eyes and attends to these needs with genuine commitment and honesty. Emily Jean literally holds onto her mother for dear life. In spite of Emily's giftedness, she develops language skills very slowly. Perhaps language is delayed because her mother anticipates her every need. As Emily grows, she feels very frustrated because preschool teachers and peers are not as attentive as her mother. Leslie struggles to understand Emily's social issues at preschool. With help from me and our parenting group and a new school for Emily Jean, Leslie learns to set limits on her love and attentiveness. She realizes that she overidentifies with her daughter, which helps her set some realistic limits. Her daughter learns to use her words and to adjust to being a part of a social group at preschool.

The parents in my group have learned that setting limits is harder after a child has been overprotected by an overidentified mother.

Rebecca was raised by nannies in a very wealthy, highly educated, well-run home. On the surface, her childhood was quite the opposite of what Leslįe experienced. She shared her thoughts about her initial experiences with her son Dylan. Interestingly, Rebecca has problems that are very similar to Leslie's: overidentification and overparenting. Rebecca wrote:

I didn't feel a sense of oneness right away, though I loved him instantly.

While this statement on the surface is confusing, it illustrates the power of a mother's need to give her child what she herself did not get from her own mother. Rebecca got everything but love. Rebecca came from a home with loads of expectations and not enough real unconditional support from her parents. She wants to give her son Dylan unconditional love, even though she is not even sure what unconditional love is. Dylan is often indulged emotionally by his doting mother. Rebecca has to learn to be more realistic about how much she needs to do for her son. Dylan, like Emily Jean, has developed unrealistic expectations of friends and teachers. Dylan withdraws when he is not the center of attention at school and on play dates. As Rebecca becomes more aware of her own overprotectiveness, her son develops better social skills. The parents in my group learned that withdrawal and shyness are common problems in gifted children who are overprotected.

There are other twists and turns that complicate the attachment between mothers and their infants. Judy, an identical twin and a parent who I helped over the years, explains:

I was a young mother right out of college with no experience with babies. I really didn't think about how close I would feel to my first child, but we were extremely close. My daughter's needs were the center of my life, similar to the closeness I felt for my twin sister.

Judy had to share her mother's love and attention with her twin sister Janet. Longing for more closeness and singular attention from her own mother, she showered her daughter Hillary with an inordinate amount of attention in an attempt to overcome her own feelings of neediness. Unconsciously, she recreated her twin bond with her daughter. Eventually, Hillary became a tyrant whose intense hour-long temper tantrums and emotional demands frightened her grandmother, aunt, brothers, father, and housekeeper. Judy had to get insight and support from me and other parents in the group to understand how to contain and calm her daughter. Judy's insight into her own overprotective behavior was an ongoing and complicated journey that started with saying "no." Setting limits based on child-centered expectations was a solution that worked for this family. The parents in my group came to understand that saying "no" is a challenging and common problem for parents of gifted children.

Clearly Leslie's, Rebecca's, and Judy's compulsive attentiveness make up for their own childhoods of emptiness and loss. These moms are giving their children what they longed for from their parents. It is very stressful for Leslie, Rebecca, and Judy to set child-centered limits for their children. When they say "no" to their son or daughter, they are unconsciously saying the same to themselves. Unfortunately, these mothers in their own well-meaning way are overparenting their children because they have difficulty drawing the line between parenting themselves and parenting their children. In these instances, setting limits is painful, confusing, and even impossible. Are you wondering who the child is? Who the parent is?

HOW TO DRAW THE LINE BETWEEN PARENT AND CHILD, AND HOW TO SET LIMITS

Setting child-centered limits is based on perceiving how you and your child are different. From the infant's normal developmental dependence on his or her parents and the emotional oneness they share, emotional boundaries naturally develop. The more parents are able to attend to who their child really is and put aside what they want for the child and for themselves, the stronger and more resilient their attachment will be with the new member of the family. Still, even with eyes wide open, limit setting is hard to understand and to carry out. Frequently, parents are totally oblivious to how their unmet childhood disappointments affect their parenting decisions.[6]

I will share some of my experiences consulting with families about how to define and set child-centered limits. I have had countless experiences with very bright and gifted children who are demanding on almost every level. I have discovered that once parents accept the challenges inherent in raising a highly spirited son or daughter and stop wishing for a perfectly calm and well-behaved child, the easier life becomes. I have so many examples of this principle of understanding and acceptance. My favorite one follows.

Jane, an extremely successful professor with a list of degrees from the finest Ivy League schools, consulted with me about school placement for Ron, her extremely intense, bright, and talented child. While Jane knew from school reports and just talking to her son that Ron had inherited some of her IQ points, she was very concerned about Ron's lack of interest at school and his "underachievement." Jane wanted her son to be an academic and a real intellectual. She hoped her son would follow in her footsteps.

After I established rapport with Jane, I was able to explain that what is unique about the intensity of gifted children and their gifted parents is the challenge of setting limits for fairness and safety. Once she understood and accepted that her son was a challenge because he saw the world through his own eyes, not hers, their relationship began to flourish. Of course, there were the normal ups and downs of growing up. Jane learned to accept and respect that her son was his own person. Making him into the ideal image of what she wanted him to be was not important. This was a difficult but valuable lesson that she had to learn and relearn.

The question raised at the beginning of the chapter about who the parent is may at first sound confusing or absurd. On a psychological and emotional level, there is crossover between the parent and the infant and growing child. This psychological reciprocity—give and take—between mother and child is understandable and makes setting limits a very real challenge.

The following questions will help you explore the issues described thus far in this chapter.

Ask yourself:

How am I emotionally different from my child and how is my child different from me?

Good enough response: My baby is very outgoing and curious. Although he is intense, I can calm him down if I follow a plan that he is familiar with. My husband and I were very difficult to calm down when we were children. My husband was an outgoing baby. I was shy and fearful, and I hid behind my mother.

Undermining response: I can see myself in my daughter's eyes. She is headstrong like me and has to be continually held. No one is able to help me calm her down. I don't think I can be a good mother to her.

What am I projecting onto my son or daughter?

Good enough response: Sometimes I can tell that I am overreacting to Dee Dee's fear of being left alone with my mother. Everything is set up and safe. In my growing years, there was so much chaos that I was always frightened when I was left with babysitters. This is a different situation for my daughter.

Undermining response: My father was a very famous man, and I always lived in his shadow. I don't want this for my son, so I am going to treat him as if he were an agent who is totally free from my family of origin. No matter what, my son has to develop a better sense of himself than I have been able to do for myself.

Who is the parent?

Good enough response: I am in charge of certain decisions about health, safety, nutrition, bedtime, and schooling. My kids can have some choices about food, clothes, toys, friends, and gifts they are interested in. I am willing to negotiate some rules in certain special situations.

Undermining response: My children will have the freedom to make as many decisions as they want to make.

THE PARENTAL DILEMMA OVER WHAT TO PROVIDE

There are practical concrete decisions to make that are not psychologically motivated. Parents' assessment of what to provide is crucial because ultimately parents make the decisions no matter how child-centered they choose to be. Parents need to develop confidence in themselves as parents. Still, parents look to the experts like me for answers. The "father knows best" era is over. The loss of extended family living in the same city as the grandchildren complicates determining who the authority on child rearing is. There are *too many* options available for concerned parents to enhance their child's emotional, physical, and intellectual abilities. Parents with absolutely pristine goals for their child can "make themselves crazy" trying to perfectly orchestrate their child's developmental potential.

To illustrate the diversity of decisions parents can make about child development, I asked mothers who work with me about how they decided on toys and play activities for their growing infants and toddlers. Here is what they had to say.

Leslie shares her reasons for selecting her children's toys: *Emily Jean didn't play with rattles or stuffed animals for very long. She was interested in household objects. Then I set my house up like a cooperative preschool. We had blocks, Legos, puzzles, and musical instruments. Emily Jean just loved her board books. We followed her lead. Sometimes we did use Baby Einstein when we needed a break.*

Leslie tries very hard to be creative and connected to her daughter's inclinations and directions. She is very successful in one sense. But her lack of concern with setting a structure for safety and follow-through on transitions and social skills is problematic. EJ is not being given a chance to develop her sense of herself with other adults and children.

Sara, an attorney, shares: *I did have idealistic ideas on how to parent. My daughter was very well planned. My theories on child rearing went out the window when Tammy was born. I could not spend time worrying about the right toys. When she was five months old, I went back to work full time, so she got to watch TV too early in life. Still, I encouraged Tammy to use her imagination and to do nondirected activities. I started reading to her very early in life, and I still read to her every day. I buy toys that reflect her interests.*

Sara is warm and gentle with her daughter. She is careful not to limit her emotional well-being with rigid rules about behavior. Her decisions reflect her belief that children need love. Sara does have difficulty balancing work and her daughter. Setting limits can be difficult for her when she feels guilty about being away from home. After a long day, Sara gives in to her daughter's demands. Giving in sets up a power struggle between mother and daughter, which makes setting limits very stressful.

Patty, a very focused mother, has a slightly different take: *We deliberately chose to limit our children's exposure to media since my husband works in TV on commercials and marketing. Other parenting ideas come from friends' choices and a book called* Baby Wise. *Since the kids were on a schedule in the NICU [neonatal intensive care unit], we continued it. The idea was very simple and also supported by Dr. Spock—eat, play, sleep.*

Patty's success with early environmental stimulation stems from her scientific and artistic sensibilities. Patty does have difficulties making decisions that cannot be pure and well thought out. Her children's emotional intensity can worry her inordinately and often leads to her difficulty with setting limits.

Leslie's, Sara's, and Patty's unique voices illustrate how a parent's ideals, deliberateness, and love shape a child's development. In addition, parenting often sets up conflicts over following directions.

Ask yourself:

Are my decisions about early childhood care just a reaction to what went wrong in my growing years?

Good enough response: I look at both the good and limited aspects of my childhood when I make a decision.

Undermining reaction: I will never do anything that my parents believed in. They are the source of all of my unhappiness.

Have I thought through my decisions and consulted with my partner?

Good enough response: My partner and I make big decisions together. But it is not possible to make all of our decisions together. It is unrealistic.

Undermining reaction: My wife makes the decisions about the kids, and I make the decisions about finances.

Am I spending money to keep up with the neighbors or to show off?

Good enough reaction: It is very hard to entirely ignore what our neighbors have. But we make decisions about our lives based on our values.

Undermining reaction: We have the nicest house in the neighborhood and the most help. We are the best!!!

DEVELOPING SUPPORT SYSTEMS HELPS PARENTS SET LIMITS AND FOLLOW THROUGH

Times have really changed since I grew up. As a child, I never remember having a baby sitter. My brother or our grandparents, aunts, and uncles took care of us when mom was helping dad at the pharmacy. My twin sister remembers that in 1973, our mother Sylvia cried from fear and humiliation when she heard that her two-year-old grandson Michael was going to day care for an hour. For my mother and her generation of parents, day care was unthinkable.

As I raised my children, Richard and Elizabeth, more mothers were returning to work, but there was still a sense of extended family. Richard and Elizabeth knew their grandparents, aunts, uncles, and cousins. Even though I was going to graduate school, I was able to be home when my kids were home. Household help allowed for some spontaneity in our family life. Rigid schedules that had to be followed in a militaristic manner were not part of my kids' lives. Only homework and bedtime were enforced strictly. Flexibility in our family structure assured my kids that their needs were important to me.

Nurturing community life and ample support systems for young families is more difficult today because more women have entered the workforce in higher-level positions that require more time away from home. With mom out of the house more and the hands-on comfort and flexibility of the extended family and grandparents disappearing, child care has become a serious issue. Young families who move to pursue careers have to seek out new supportive and reliable caregivers. Early socialization that used to be taken care of more naturally by the extended family or neighborhood has been replaced by day care and early schooling.

New critical understandings from child development research suggests that emotional and social intelligence requires early and active encouragement. Parents have legitimate concerns about providing appropriate socialization for their very young children. Mom and Dad attend parent-child groups such as Mommy and Me or Daddy and Me. Play dates have become an essential part of the family routine because, theoretically, early social experiences lead to higher social and emotional intelligence.[7] In-house caregivers and nannies are asked to attend parenting classes so that they can talk to children in an appropriate tone and interact with developmental savvy. Books are written by and for grandparents to keep these traditional bastions of wisdom updated. But old-fashioned wisdom is rarely honored, which can be positive but is often negative. Good enough parenting is hard for young parents to understand and embrace because the payoff is hard to understand unless one is very psychologically minded. Competition between parents can blindside common sense.

WHO SHOULD I LISTEN TO?

Fathers and mothers today have to develop their own family-like support systems. Parenting groups run by schools and private consultants provide useful information and emotional support for new families. Advice from schools and their experts can be important, or it can be flat-out wrong. Always consult an outside independent evaluator when your child has problems at school. Make sure that the expert you are working with is really an expert. I am not advising doctor shopping, but listening to suspect advices is a problem.

Helpful Expert Advice

Linda, who has attended my parenting groups for more than five years, shared the following story: *Our son was very difficult to calm down, and making a real connection with him was extremely difficult. Carl was not developing social skills. Our pediatrician suggested an evaluation by a developmental pediatrician, who diagnosed our son as being on the autism spectrum. Having an understanding of what we were dealing with was critical. We have followed the advice of professionals to help our son overcome his "shyness." We have been successful with the help of his teachers and individuals on our support team.*

Linda was terrified when she learned that Carl might be on the autism spectrum. She immediately thought the worst. Carl would never grow up to be an independent adult. Linda conscientiously explored and evaluated all of the options for behavioral interventions that promote social development in young children. She successfully established a working plan to help Carl at the regional center for children with developmental disabilities in the city she lived in. Speech therapists and floor time therapists (behavioral therapists who worked with Carl to develop social skills) were very successful in helping Carl function at a prestigious private school. Linda's emotional struggles were intense but directed toward positive goals for her son. Keeping her eye on her son's growing social confidence got Linda through moments of helplessness and despair. Moving forward and not giving into her negativity helped Linda develop her son's potential. As I write this book, Carl is a shy teenager who is able to fit in at school with his friends. He is a high achiever, a strong athlete, and ambitious about going to college.

Bad Advice from Experts

Unlike Linda, Rebecca had an unfortunate experience at her son's preschool that is all too common. Teachers and principals suggested that Dylan was on the autism spectrum. She reports: *Our religious preschool did not know how to deal with my son's curiosity. Dylan did not want to go to school, which led my husband and me to have serious arguments about Dylan going to school anyway. When Dylan was at school, he had trouble making friends. He would wander around aimlessly. In the classroom, he was often disengaged and daydreaming. The preschool suggested that Dylan was on the autism spectrum. The head of the school wanted us to consult with a developmental pediatrician. My husband wanted us to stick it out, worrying about what the community at our temple would say if we left. When I finally got the courage to change schools, Dylan was unbelievably relieved. And so was I. The diagnosis of autism spectrum disorder was never brought up again. Dylan was very engaged at a progressive developmental preschool, although he daydreams like other children who are imaginatively intense. Dylan is doing well academically and socially.*

Parents today have to devote a great deal of energy to developing an extended family structure, which includes the child's school, for emotional and practical support. Creating a social structure is an intensely difficult and stressful problem. There are profound and substantial rewards; the payoff is a better home life and more flexibility for kids and parents alike. Having an attentive support system helps parents set limits they can follow. When your support system does not understand your gifted parenting problem, your life is more complicated, and you can lose confidence as a parent.

My best advice on developing your social network is to follow your own intuitive sense of the problem. This does not mean worrying or obsessing. Remember, no school, babysitter, grandparent, or spouse is a perfect mirror for your concerns. Establish realistic expectations for people who help you. This does not mean you should ignore your problems if you are disappointed in people who help you. You need to learn to communicate your concerns and have shared goals that are evaluated and re-evaluated.

Ask yourself:

Am I carefully working on developing a support system for my child?

Good enough reaction: Slowly, but surely, I am finding people who understand our family issues and can follow and endorse the way we parent our children. My support system is wide enough so that I have options if I need to use them.

Undermining reaction: I am doing everything myself. I cannot find anyone who lives up to my standards.

Do I make an effort to see our family and friends who dearly love my child?

Good enough reaction: We have a large family who can makes us feel guilty if we don't make it to every family event. To keep our relationship loving, we have set limits on how much time we spend visiting our families. We always try for quality family time.

Undermining reaction: We never visit our families because they are just too high maintenance. We take time off only to go to great resorts or on business ventures. Family is not important to us.

THE LEGACY OF A PARENT'S CHILDHOOD AFFECTS DISCIPLINE: THE ABILITY TO SET LIMITS

Setting limits is a serious challenge for parents of gifted children. At the expense of repeating myself, what is less understood and talked about is the effect of unconscious parental limitations in relationship to discipline. In other words, deeply buried, almost forgotten issues can blindside parents. Unresolved parental conflicts, which are manifested in ways such as poor self-esteem or a grandiose sense of self, become strong determinants of parenting style. In general, parents who have idealized their son or daughter will see their adult children turn into know-it-all grownups. The reverse is also true. Parents who are overbearing and critical will have adult children who are insecure and lacking in conviction when it comes to making their own decisions about their lives and their children.

What parents do to compensate for the deficiencies in their own childhoods is a form of self-reparenting as they provide corrective emotional experiences for their child. A father who was deprived of family closeness as a child might ensure that his "new" family spends time together on holidays. And he may fail to set up necessary downtime for himself. Making up for his own losses as well as giving a sense of closeness and continuity to his children can override his own happiness. Likewise, a father who values consumerism, because he grew up poor, will most likely have a son who values hands-on time with his own children and handmade presents.

The new mother whose parents bitterly divorced will likely vow to never leave her husband in an attempt to save her children from the same suffering that she experienced from the breakup of her family of origin. Understanding general issues such as divorce, alcoholism, child abuse, poverty, and the loss of a parent will provide a framework for mothers and fathers to make life choices for their children.

Parents who attend my support groups had these experiences to share about how their own childhood relationships shaped their parenting choices.

Leslie writes: *My mother and father had terrible childhoods. There were no examples of good parenting to help them raise us, so it is no surprise that I didn't agree with the way my mother raised me. She would let my brother and I cry it out. The drama in our family was over money, not us. Although she was very loving, she was very strict. She did not change her approach to meet our emotional needs.*

Leslie had to learn to reduce the drama at her home that developed over "too much attention." Because of her genuine open-mindedness she has overcome her own inclination to overparent.

Patty reiterates her convictions to be a little more than her own mother: *I hope I am a different parent than my mother. She resented our very being, the responsibilities of motherhood, and sharing my father's riches with her daughter and grandchildren. She was incredibly narcissistic and though she loved, she did not love unconditionally.*

Patty is an indulgent mother. She is always in danger of being a micromanager because she does not see her own overparenting. Fortunately, she is a very insightful mother who has to work very hard to set limits and to provide structure for her children. As she begins to understand her own insecurities about her childhood and resolve them with time and experiences, Patty makes wiser decisions about how to parent. Setting limits for her children remains extremely stressful and unnatural for her.

Rebecca says: *I am the opposite of my mother as a parent. I knew from the time I was a young child that I would treat my own child differently. My mother was extremely negative, critical, and cold, and she yelled all the time. She was emotionally abusive throughout my childhood.*

Rebecca has a great deal of difficulty making decisions about the best way to bring up her son. She has a graduate degree in child development, and other parents consult her. Rebecca can be blind to her own insecurities, which are based on her mother's criticalness. Her need to please her family, husband, and child to avoid conflict is deep rooted and very tenacious. Because of Rebecca's emotionally deprived childhood, she cannot trust her own decisions. Rebecca needs affirmation about how well she is parenting. She eagerly reaches out for help and advice, which is an adaptive coping strategy.

Ann, still angry at her mother, does not mince words: *Well, I am not a raging alcoholic for one, so I feel pretty good about that. My mother was also very self-centered and negative, and I'm not even sure she really wanted to have children at all. She was not available emotionally either. She was a stay at home mom. It really was all about her, although she would remind us constantly how much she "worried" about us. Though that seems still all about her when I think of it. I am so very concerned that my children get the attention they need from me.*

Ann cannot see her blind spots as a parent because of the chaos of her childhood. Gradually, with help from a psychotherapist, she is learning who she is as a mother. Learning that mothers are entitled to have their own lives is critical. Her blind spot that keeps her from taking care of herself is receding as Ann sees that her children don't need to be attended to continually.

Conflicted feelings about the quality of parenting and unresolved childhood issues established a framework for child rearing choices for Leslie, Patty, Rebecca, and Ann. Insight into the useful and limited aspects of their growing years gives these moms a way of looking at their parenting roles. As these mothers gain knowledge about the complexity of parenting, they make better choices. Setting limits for their intense sons and daughters creates less anxiety, and parental directives have more conviction. Fortunately, children who understand that there are rules and structure in their lives develop a better sense of self and are more secure.

In conclusion, more deeply rooted childhood traumas or neglect can easily be overlooked or ignored, haunting the most well-meaning parent. Past childhood ghosts can create life problems that are hard to understand, to defuse, and to put to rest. Unfortunately but understandably, blind spots disrupt effective parenting. For example, a devoted mother may protect her child from the pressure she experienced to achieve in school by selecting a warm and nurturing educational environment. But she may be unaware of her poor self-esteem and inability to be assertive with her husband, boss, and—yes—her child. On a mission to heal or overcome her childhood nightmares, the attentive mother fixates on the obvious but misses the undertow of her poor self-esteem.

Ask yourself:

Do I have any blind spots as a parent?

Good enough response: Yes, I am sure that I do. I try to look beyond my own negativity, which masks the fears that are mine and not my child's.

Undermining response: No, I see the world and my family in black and white. I make decisions based on what I see.

Can I see the whole picture of who my child may grow up to be?

Good enough response: My child will evolve into the person he wants to be. I can see strengths and issues that pop up each and every day, which I attend to directly.

Undermining response: I *know* I want my child to follow in my footsteps, so I am giving him a childhood similar to my own.

Do I avoid making decisions or setting limits because I am afraid of conflict?

Good enough response: Sometimes I do avoid making decisions to keep the peace at home. But I really don't use avoidance as a way to handle conflict.

Undermining response: We have rigid rules that we follow regarding conflicts.

PERFECT PARENTS OF GIFTED CHILDREN HAVE GREAT DIFFICULTY SETTING LIMITS

Inadequate parenting occurs when parents place their needs for closeness and sharing before their child's needs.[8,9] "Emotional theft" and the "false self" are outgrowths of inadequate or narcissistic parenting.[10] They are common mistakes of "perfect" parents. While the good enough parent is emotionally available to understand what their child feels and needs, they are able to make adult decisions and set limits because they know that understanding does not always lead to giving in. Good enough parents are able to try new ways of relating to their child without the fear of making a mistake.

Narcissistically invested parents think that making a mistake will have devastating consequences for their child. In their carefulness, overinvolved parents can raise children who are prone to dependence and fragility. Overparenting can lead to raising a child who lacks resilience. For the sake of their children as well as themselves, mothers and fathers need to learn to say "no."

Learning when to stop taking care of your son or daughter and to take care of yourself, your relationship with your spouse, or your career means drawing a line in the sand between your own identity and your child's identity. Deciding where to draw the line and establish emotional boundaries is vital, deep rooted, and very complicated. Deciding what your child needs, what you want to give, and what you need to give to "overcome" and heal yourself colors your choices. To illustrate this profound idea, I asked the parents in my support group why they had problems drawing the line or setting limits.

Britney writes: *Yes, limits are difficult. My husband, who is not psychologically minded, tends to bring the hammer down with no warning, resulting in chaos. I try hearing my husband's and son's concerns, and I give in when my son's request is reasonable.*

The problem Britney faces is that she and her husband are not on the same page. Their son Jason is getting mixed messages about what he is entitled to. Mom is consistent and concerned about setting limits, but dad undermines his wife's decisions and confuses his son. While both parents agree on most issues, school choice and discipline are areas of conflict. There is potential in the family for deep-seated unhappiness.

Sara, a cardiologist, has difficulty being consistent with her daughter. Her mother was seriously depressed, so Sara felt devalued because there was not enough love. In turn, Sara always wants to mirror her child's feelings. She reports: *It is hard for me to set limits because I work. I want my daughter to spend good happy quality time with me. I talk with her a lot and try to verbalize her reactions to me when I do say no.*

Sara goes too far with her patience and good listening skills. She struggles to focus on her own needs. In general, Sara lets her daughter and husband get away with unacceptable emotional and unruly behavior. Sara often becomes overwhelmed and then thinks her only option is to run away from home. As she learns to say no firmly, her family's problems become more manageable.

Ann writes: *When I do draw the line, which is really hard, I have to stick to my guns no matter how emotional Evan gets. And that is hard for me to bear as a mom. Because I don't want to see my child so upset. But I try to tell myself that hearing no is actually good for him. And he must play by the rules in life and in my house.*

Ann gets lost setting limits because of her own chaotic childhood. As she reports, setting limits is enormously scary and perhaps even confusing. Ann sees her own pain too clearly in her son's eyes. Ann suffers from depression. As Ann gets help to feel better about herself with a mental health professional, she begins to have an easier time saying no.

Obviously, Leslie, Sara, and Ann, who attend my parenting groups, are concerned about being empathetic with their children and are afraid to be "strict." Still, they understand that the maintenance of their own sanity is possible only when they enforce reasonable rules for their children, husbands, and homes. Because they all have very bright and emotionally intense children, setting limits is not easy. It is necessary for parents to accept that arguing is often second nature to extremely bright children. Getting bright children to understand that there are parental decisions that only parents make is also a key to sanity.

Ask yourself:

Do I have some rules for safety that I stick to no matter what?

Good enough response: Yes, we do have certain rules for safety. Sometimes we make an exception if we have a special occasion that calls for some flexibility.

Undermining response: We have taught our children about what is safe and what is not safe. We allow them to make their own decisions in this regard.

Has giving in become an easy way out for me?

Good enough response: No, not really. I do give in sometimes when it is a special event or time of the year.

Undermining reaction: I am very open minded. I give my children choices because I did not get any growing up. I am proud to say that there are 15 flavors of ice cream in my freezer.

Are limits really that hard for gifted children to understand?

Good enough response: Yes, gifted kids are very persistent. They need a lot of re-enforcement and structure to learn to follow the rules we value.

Undermining reaction: I don't want my gifted children to become robots or just good little soldiers. So I let them find their own limits as much as possible.

Does my husband help me discipline our children in a consistent way?

Good enough response: While my spouse and I cannot be clones of one another when we give our children direction or explain our expectations, we agree on a philosophy of discipline. We back each other up as much as is possible.

Undermining reaction: We each have our own styles for setting limits. We are divorced. We do not fight in front of our children, but we cannot agree to support one another. Our children will have to live with this inconsistency and our mixed messages.

CONTEMPORARY ISSUES THAT AFFECT SETTING UP THE EMOTIONAL FENCES

Seriously, this debate over who is the parent is not only absurd but dangerous. Mothers and fathers are in charge of deciding the structure of their child's life, even though parent-child identity is intertwined and the gifted child thinks he or she knows it all. The child is dependent on his or her parents for life-sustaining care. In turn, parents are dependent on their child's state of mind and sense of well-being to feel good about themselves as caretakers. Well-intentioned good enough parents longing for smooth sailing often have blurred vision when deciding where to establish the emotional fences that separate an adult decision from a child decision. If they can't say no, good enough parents need to put their own insecurity in the hands of a good psychotherapist.

Common boundary issues based on a lack of clarity about who is the parent are blatantly apparent when parents and kids fight over the house rules: who decides what is for dinner, what televisions programs are acceptable, and when it's time to brush teeth and go to bed.

Besides dealing with the ghosts of their own childhoods, new parents have difficult choices to make for other reasons. New parents have to make decisions about the scope of their responsibilities. Very often, new parents have to give up their own real personal comfort and routines such as sleeping seven hours and working on challenging careers (which can promote self-esteem) to develop a strong emotional connection with their infant. Once on this track of giving up their comfort zones, parents lose sight of the reality of their own needs. Parenting can easily become a career to succeed at, instead of a role in your whole well-rounded all-encompassing life.

In an effort to do the best they can, some of the new mothers and fathers I meet with have read as many books as they can find about child development. Knowing developmental milestones and methods for raising a healthy child is obviously helpful in many areas. Yet, the intuitive process that parents have to develop through trial and error can be neglected or eliminated. *Yes, making mistakes is very important.* Parents have to find out what works for them, and sometimes, they even have to learn *how* to discover what is effective.

Jenny and Frank, described at the start of this chapter, could be candidates for doctorates in child development. These savvy parents are informed and knowledgeable. Their verbal skills are stellar. They communicate non-stop with their children Michael and Harry about every behavior and interaction. Mom often remarks with empathy and compassion, "I can see you are _____ " (bored, tired, hungry, frustrated, unhappy). Does she now give in? Of course not.

Mirroring your child's feelings is only the first step: "Oh, I can see you are angry." Then it is followed up by: "It is time to put away your toys. You can play after lunch." Does she give up? Of course not. Jenny sticks to the child-centered family rules.

Talking about everything with your child has replaced establishing realistic rules. Your family rules should be based on your own values and your sense of yourself as a parent. When children understand what is and what is not acceptable, their lives are calmer, more stable, and more predictable. Sharing too much of your thinking about why you have made certain rules can be very confusing for gifted kids because in turn they will try to negotiate a new settlement, which is, of course, not possible anyway.

Here are a few questions to ask yourself that will help you set up realistic practical and emotional limits—or, as psychologists call them, boundaries—for your bright and challenging child. Obviously, there are no single-sentence answers that will tell you how to draw the line establishing a boundary between acceptable and not acceptable. A strong identity as a parent will help you create a home environment that will foster collaboration and problem solving between you and your child. With good will between parent and child that is based on establishing realistic fences, your family life will be more understandable and subject to fewer temper tantrums, frustrations, and traumatic circumstances.

What are my expectations for raising a gifted child?

This is a very serious question. Your answer will be the foundation of how you parent your children in their early lives as well as when they are teenagers. Yes, when your children are adults, they will still look to you for emotional support. You should try to be as honest as you can with yourself. If you think having children is always going to be a lot of fun, you are sure to be frustrated and unhappy with your children at some point.

If you can't bear to come up with fantasies or expectations about raising children, most likely you are unprepared for the havoc kids can create. Lack of expectations from mom and dad can often lead to permissive parenting. When children create their own individuality without parental input, their sense of self lacks resilience. Parental wisdom and judgment help children grow.

Good enough response:

I expect that having children will be rewarding and challenging. I have spent some time thinking about what I want for my children in terms of education, family time, travel, and extras.

Undermining responses:

- Whatever happens will happen. Their fate is not in my hands.
- I don't have expectations. My parents had so many rules that I feel my life was stilted, and I was smothered.
- I want the structure of our lives to develop solely from our attachment to each other. We will be a close-knit family who sticks together.
- My children will do exactly as they are told!

A plan that can be evaluated and revised is what you need. An adequate statement of your expectations for raising a child will require understanding child development and applying these theories. Even a little knowledge of normal development is better than none. Having knowledgeable experts will help you as well.

A very permissive approach is inadequate and undermines your child's development. Self-esteem is distorted when the child is given too much power. Obviously, rigidity stifles the child's evolving self and seriously limits his or her confidence.

How will I be different as a parent from my mother and father in regards to discipline?

The answer to this question is complicated. You will have to look at what your parents did that was valuable. Like the parents I work with, you must think about *what* you want to do differently than your mother and father. There are countless examples of new parents reacting to parenting based on their childhood experiences. I shared some of these reactions at the beginning of this chapter. Holding on to the good and reworking the negative is critical.

Good enough responses:

- I will learn from my parents' mistakes and my own mistakes.
- I will learn about the issues that mothers and fathers face by reading and thinking about what the experts say.
- I will make my own decisions based on the facts and what is practical for my family.
- I will accept what I cannot change.

Undermining responses:

- I want to be a perfect parent.
- I will absolutely follow the advice of experts.

If you want to be a perfect parent, I assure you this is a road to unhappiness and an emotionally chaotic family life. Ask yourself these questions first: Why do you value perfection, and what does it represent to you? What happens when perfection cannot be achieved? How do you deal with the imperfections of other people that you encounter? Was your mother perfect? Did she want you to be perfect?

Practice being imperfect. It might make your day.

What values do I want to give my children that they can take with them as they travel through their lives?

This is a crucial issue. What you want your children to value will come from your own beliefs. Love, truth, creativity, honor, duty, prosperity, belief in God, kindness, orderliness, aesthetics, skill, and intellectual curiosity are common values that individuals aspire toward. Make your own list and teach your children those values. Clarity in the realm of what you value will give your fence building conviction.

Good enough response:

I will examine the values of my family of origin and with respect, redefine what is important to me and my family.

Undermining responses:

- We will follow with great devotion the rules that I grew up with.
- I want my children to decide for themselves.

Who can help me raise my children with the emotional boundaries that are important to me?

Optimally, you will have your partner/spouse as a co-facilitator and a longstanding consultant who supports your parenting plan. You will also need hands-on help to keep your household in some type of order. Don't blindly rely on your mother or your aunt. Make a serious plan for outside help that reinforces the structure you believe in.

Good enough response:

I will have to balance my work schedule with good enough child care. Sharing child rearing responsibilities with my partner is a must.

Undermining response:

I *have* to work, so my child will *have* to go to child care or to my parents.

CONCLUDING IDEAS: YOU ARE IN CHARGE

Understanding yourself and examining *why* you are acting and reacting to your child is your most important tool. The problem of how to establish rules to run your household is very challenging. Although some experts will give you easy rules to follow, I know that there are no short easy answers or rigid standards that can provide the right or perfect solution with gifted children. Without a doubt, understanding who you are as a parent will help you draw compassionate lines between action and inaction.

Always remember, *you are the parent.* Have conviction about saying "no." As the parent, you are your child's most important decision maker. Your child will learn from your compassion and wisdom how to make decisions for himself or herself.

RARITAN VALLEY COMMUNITY COLLEGE
EVELYN S. FIELD LIBRARY

4

How to Live with Your Smart Child's Intensity

It is never ending. Continuous. Endless questions, introspection, analysis, and a hot energy that prevails during the daytime and into the night. My son's intensity extends to relationships with friends, teachers, tutors, doctors, coaches, and, of course, family. Paul possess a deep need to be in control and controlling as he tries to force his ideas on others, yet at the same time, he has an equal interest in caring for and nurturing others. My son has an intense need to find his place in the world. He is a negotiator who wants what is right for other people in his life.
—*Erin*

YOUR GIFTED CHILD'S INTENSITY IS A NORMAL BEHAVIORAL CHARACTERISTIC

Learning to deal with the emotional intensity of a smart and talented child or adolescent takes a lot of energy, time, patience, and understanding. Eventually, parents learn to accept their son's or daughter's emotional quirkiness. Parents, teachers, and behavioral, occupational, and health therapists all need to keep in mind that cognitive strength and cognitive complexity give rise to emotional depth. Profound feelings come out of the hearts and minds of gifted children that the child or adolescent needs to express or rather, is compelled to talk about in detail. Smart children who have high IQs or creative talents not only think differently—more quickly and profoundly—but their feeling states have a more vivid and encompassing quality of intensity that needs to be expressed and listened to.[1,2] For example, when preschoolers say goodbye to their parents, they often behave as if they are falling apart. They easily imagine that their parents will never return. But eventually, they do calm down.

As another example, consider that when young gifted children see a homeless person, they feel and think that they need to save him or her or to solve the problem with homelessness. You need to explain that homelessness is not a problem that children can solve.

From reading and watching movies about racehorses, I liken the process of parenting a gifted kid to training a high-strung race horse. I say this because as smart and as precocious as kids are is unfortunately—or fortunately (depending on your state of mind)—as intense as they may become in any given situation that triggers emotional confusion and stress. The stallion needs a horse whisperer, and the gifted child needs a parent whisperer. Calming down and refocusing the emotionally intense child is a serious challenge. It is truly a steep learning curve that parents have to navigate as they try to give their children the tools they need to reach their potential. Truly and obviously, there is no one size fits all direction for all parents to take with their gifted kids. There are no recipes to follow. But in general, along with calmness and structure at home, appropriate schooling and socialization are crucial tools that help contain emotional intensity. It is not as easy for parents of gifted kids to find a school and social match as it is for the neighbors' children who have an easier time fitting in.

While the intensity of spirited smart children is common and predictable, the degree of their emotional reactivity can be confusing to parents, teachers, and specialists. In a desperate attempt to end the confusion about emotional reactivity, the gifted child with problems is often misunderstood and mislabeled with a psychiatric diagnosis. Books and Internet articles are written on the differences between gifted children, autism spectrum disorder, and attention deficit disorder because children who have intense feelings are singled out because they have difficult to handle emotional and behavioral problems.[3]

However, the social-emotional and learning issues of gifted children are very different from those of children with autism or hyperactivity. Correct diagnostic labels are critical because they prescribe the school and home environment that best fits the child's special learning needs.[4] For example, boredom in smart children who are perfectionists may lead to underachievement. Most parents, teachers, and administrators do not understand that boredom in gifted kids is common when they are not in the right school environment. Teachers and administrators very often misunderstand underachievement as the child just not being as smart as his or her parents think. Socialization issues such as difficulty making friends and getting bullied are very common but evolve out of feeling misunderstood by peers, not developmental delays related to autism spectrum disorder.[5]

Spirited children's sensitivity to people and events around them can be disarming to the uninformed and uneducated teacher, caregiver, grandparent, or any other person who gets a glimpse of the intense feelings and "over the top behavior." The smart and spirited kid's behavior and mood is often called over-reactive and lacking in perspective because of the depth of feelings that are manifested in response to a simple situation. "Harry, you need to brush your teeth now" can become an opportunity for war with his parents if Harry does not want to stop what he is doing. Likewise, "Jack, you need to complete your schoolwork" can become a totally nonsensical position for a parent to take if the child finds homework boring or meaningless. "Sofia, let's turn out the lights and go to bed" is an impossible task if Sofia suffers from intense separation anxiety and truly believes that she cannot be alone.

And to make matters worse and more confusing for parents of quick and astute children, the children actually know when they are creating problems and do want to stop and help out mom or dad. Temporarily, their reasonable and empathetic behavior allows their parent to feel relieved and happy about the calm situation. Exhausted and frustrated parents have a glimmer of hope and think their children are not manipulative tyrants. Harry decides he can brush his teeth. Jack gets started on his homework. Sofia goes to sleep in her own room. The roller coaster is on the level part of the track. But quickly, the child forgets to be reasonable and reverts to his or her original position, wanting his or her own way. Graceful behavior goes by the wayside. And tyrannical attitudes take over again. Parents are better off if they accept that intense feelings create moodiness and unreasonable behaviors.

CALM YOURSELF AND YOUR GIFTED CHILD DOWN

Learning to calm down your spirited child is so difficult and yet is imperative. Curiosity and passionate beliefs that range from believing that mom or dad is wrong to wanting to understand astrophysics, specifically black holes, need to be addressed and tamed or redirected. Wishing your son or daughter were less curious is a waste of your time, and it is a thankless position to take. Parents who wish their child were less of a challenge and more normal are unfortunately very common. Whether or not parents come out and say it, I believe that all parents of gifted kids just want normal children. And this wish is their first challenge to overcome.

The parents I work with in my support group explain their experiences with their high-strung children and suggest coping strategies to help them be more realistic about what is normal when their gifted high-strung child is unhappy and feeling very intense frustration.

1. Normalize your child's over-reactivity.
Rebecca says, *Dylan is intense with everything from learning to food to friends and family. He has a heightened sense of his surroundings and a passion for whatever he enjoys. On the flip side, he has great disdain for what*

he hates and can react very strongly if he is unhappy. I have had to work with him to help him temper his responses. I have helped him understand when it is appropriate to share his feelings.

Rebecca has put a great deal of careful thought into understanding her reactions and actions with her son, Dylan. She has overcome her wish that Dylan would be a normal child who liked every play date and was eager to be a part of a sports team. As Rebecca accepted her son's temperament and passion, Dylan became easier to deal with on a day-to-day basis. Still, Dylan is a challenging child who wants what he wants and knows his own mind. Setting clear limits on his negative or inappropriate behavior has helped the family move forward.

Rebecca's quest to normalize her son's behavior for herself and for her son has been extremely effective. For example, like many gifted children, Dylan was afraid to participate in his school's winter performance. Instead of insisting that he just do it, an option to not perform was presented as reasonable and acceptable. Rebecca told Dylan that some children are not ready to perform, and it is normal to be afraid and just want to watch. The entire family and Dylan's teachers were spared the tantrums that would have taken place during the performance. The very next year, Dylan was able to perform in the school play, and he did beautifully.

2. Back off your tendency to be a perfect parent.

Rene says, *The hardest part of Monica's intensity has been finding appropriate ways to deal with her overwhelming emotions. We have had such a hard time finding ways to* not *escalate tantrums or overemphasize her fears. We had to learn to accept her intensities so that we could dial them down instead of making them worse. Giving her rewards for appropriate behavior has helped.*

Rene was at first sure that there was something "really wrong" with Monica, even though her husband reassured her that as a child, he was very much like his daughter. Gradually, like all of the mothers and fathers I work with, Rene came to understand that she just felt overwhelmed by her daughter's energy and intensity. Gradually, de-escalating tantrums and accepting that her daughter was not *normal* but gifted started to help her relax and take a different perspective. Gaining confidence in herself as a mother also helped her deal with her daughter's perfectionistic and demanding behavior.

Rene is an overdoing parent who wanted to be the perfect mother. Her initial expectation to raise perfect children was hard to give up. She had a great deal of difficulty being realistic about what was necessary. Her standards were too high. Rene worked hard to accept the idea that good enough was better than being perfect when it came to parenting. Holding on to be being a good enough parent was emotionally difficult for her. Rene had to give up her perfectionist tendencies, but she can still easily have a relapse and expect too much.

3. Hold onto your authority as a parent.

June says, *Lee's intense curiosity challenges my intellect and my patience. I have to be hyperfocused to answer all of his questions when he challenges me. He is always many questions ahead of me, anticipating my answers and developing new arguments depending on which answer I give. In minutes, I am tied in knots. I can't say "no" until we are so both upset that it really cannot end well for either of us.*

June was way too interested in being overly responsive to her son. Lee became dependent on her for the feedback and understanding that teachers and friends were unable to give with such deep attentiveness. This type of overinvolvement is a very common problem between mother and gifted child. Unraveling the interdependency between June and Lee became a very difficult process that began with June becoming more sure of herself as a mother and not so threatened by her son's critical comments. June had to learn to set very firm limits for Lee. And Lee had to learn to respect authority. With the help of psychotherapy, June came to understand that she was too involved with her son's feelings. Staying focused on specific goals and consistent parenting was a lesson that June learned gradually. Maintaining firm convictions solved many problematic situations.

School phobia and problems with authority figures intensified in adolescence as Lee felt more insecure and more embroiled in his anger at his mother. Separation anxiety can be very common in adolescence. This generalized intense anxiety is extremely difficult to contend with, especially in gifted children who always think that they know it all.

4. Establish your credibility even when it seems impossible.

Erin and Paul had close intellectual rapport. Erin shares her struggles: *Paul was my first child later in life, and he was a dynamo. I loved his ability to think through a situation and to talk about how he was thinking and feeling. I encouraged his creativity, and his father was very concerned with exposing him to great literature and ideas about art. When Paul went to school, he did not fit in with the other children. He liked to be with adults he could talk with. Kids his age bullied him. Paul thought that was an expert on how to react to bullies at age five. He was undersocialized, and he had difficulty making friends. We could not find the right school for him to attend for many years. Paul did not know how to learn like other children. His asynchronous development led specialists to believe he was hyperactive or on the autism spectrum. Seeing Paul through the lens of giftedness was the most useful and effective strategy.*

Giving up was, thankfully, not in Erin's nature. Finally, after three years, she found a private school that was able to work with Paul. Unlike the arguments that June and Lee were involved in, Erin and Paul shared a relationship that was not filled with animosity. Paul did not bully his mother. Erin had to learn that she was in charge of decisions about homework follow-though. She had to try, like many parents with gifted kids, to help her son fit in by endorsing more appropriate social skills in everyday situations. Going to the principal's office and calling mom to ask if he could come home from school early was not acceptable. Inviting the other kids in his class for play dates was encouraged. The teachers and administrators at the new private school worked to develop class camaraderie. Gradually, Paul learned to fit in with his classmates. His social development was a long and emotionally charged process for everyone involved.

When parents endorse the following strategies, they become more effective managers of issues related to the intensities of gifted children.

1. Normalize your child's intensity by accepting how profound your child feels his or her experience really is. Try to find other children's experiences that are similar. Sharing other similar experiences is soothing and calming for the gifted child.
2. Really try to back off on your tendency to be perfect parents, as this will really reduce the gifted child's tendency to withdraw into his or her intensities.
3. Hold onto your authority as parents with child centered goals.
4. Establish your credibility as the expert on your child, no matter how difficult this may be with teachers, administrators, grandparents, and spouses.

THE FIVE DIFFERENT TYPES OF INTENSITY AND OVEREXCITIBILITIES

Heightened sensitivity to people and their environment is a behavioral characteristic of gifted children. However, emotional intensity and overexcitability are also positively and extremely unique in each and every precocious child. Intense interests and passions take different paths depending on the type of intensity the child is born with.[6,7] While activity, energy, emotionality, distractability, anxiety, and moodiness are always present in a gifted child, not every gifted child learns to read at an early age. Some gifted kids are communicators and cannot stop talking. Some draw with skill way above their chronological age and do not want to stop. Music, sports, ethical issues, storytelling, computers, and electronics are also areas in which children can exhibit early intense learning abilities and talents.

Overexcitabilities is a term used to explain the intensity or superinvolvement of gifted children. In reaction to the unravelling of developmental processes, as well as environmental and educational inputs, overexcitability is the tendency and capacity to be superstimulated for long periods of time, very deeply and intensely. It is a subjective quality of experience that is vivid, absorbing, penetrating, encompassing, and complex. Overexcitabilities are a positive force for gifted children because they feed, enrich, empower, and amplify their talents and special gifts. Parents, teachers, and other specialists need to be aware of what type of intensity the gifted child is motivated and energized by. Understanding the child's uniqueness allows you to nurture and nourish his or her specialness. With awareness of the areas of difficulty that arise out of understanding intensity, it is possible for parents and teachers to differently nurture strengths and address problem areas.[8] When the details of asynchronous development are acknowledged, the whole child is nourished. For example, a child who is intellectually intense may learn to read very early but be unable to draw or participate comfortably in sports. If areas of weakness such as in sports or handwriting are ignored, the learning problem will become harder to manage. As another example, an imaginably intense child may be able to create fabulous stories, but she can be totally disinterested in math and reading. Underachievement needs to be worked on along with imaginative potential.

Overexcitability or a subjectively different ability to comprehend on an inner level certain types of thoughts, feelings, sounds, and visual perception is part of the gifted child's personality. According to Dabrowski, there are five categories of overexcitabilities[9] that are innate and depend on environmental stimulation. Parents cannot teach any of these intensities to their infant or child. A need for perfectionism is most likely to be present in areas in which the child is intense and excitable.

Psychomotor Overexcitability

Psychomotor overexcitability involves a surplus of energy, restlessness, and curiosity. The toddler, child, or adolescent who is always exploring, asking endless questions, and getting by with very little sleep demonstrates psychomotor intensity and overexcitability. Intensely driven to be active, these individuals can be restless. Often compulsive talkers, they may always be chatting about something big or small. Nervous habits such biting their nails or playing with their hair is common when they feel too confined. Psychomotor activity is very creatively driven across different types of actives. Often, this intense need to be active is mislabeled as attention deficit disorder. Hallmarks of psychomotor overexcitability include:

1. Competitiveness that can lead to impulsivity
2. Energy to move all of the time
3. Restlessness when the child has to sit still

The choice of school for a child with psychomotor sensitivity should, if possible, involve an educational philosophy that is nontraditional because the child will have difficulty sitting still all the time.

Sensual/Aesthetic Overexcitability

An overexcitability to sensual, sensory, and aesthetic pleasure is manifested as touching, tasting, hearing, being in nature, and viewing artistic objects or events being experienced more intensely than in individuals whose sensitivity to sensory, sensual, or aesthetic input is in the normal range. Tags in the back of pajamas and T-shirts drive these children crazy. A serious fondness for calamari or other exotic foods, crying when they have to leave a concert or favorite movie or book, and love of artistic activities are indications of this type of intensity. The use of language as expressed through poetry can be very compelling for individuals who are sensitive to sensual and aesthetic overexcitability. Music and dramatic performances are always uplifting for these individuals.

My daughter, Elizabeth, has aesthetic intensity that was expressed when she was a child as a continual need to redecorate her bedroom. To this very day, she is very sensitive to her environment and driven to create an aesthetic that meets her imagination of how things look. Similarly, a child that I worked with was continually drawing people and their clothing. Later, she studied fashion design and became well known in her field.

There are other forms of this type of intensity. Sometimes, children with sensory intensity over-react to noise in their environment. They are often involved with occupational therapy to help them cope with their noise issues. Unfortunately, children with sensory issues are too often said to be on the autism spectrum or overly fearful, when in actuality, their sensitivities are a sign of giftedness.

Hallmarks of sensual overexcitability include:

1. Extreme sensitivity to colors, shapes, designs and textures, tastes, and beauty
2. A love of listening to sounds of nature and a feeling of connectedness with animals and plants
3. Feeling moved and inspired by artistic experiences

Educational choices for these children should include schools that value artistic production and creativity. An open-ended curriculum that looks at diversity of responses is critical. Opportunities for art, music, and dramatics is also crucial.

Intellectual Overexcitability

Intellectual intensity is seen in interests and strong signs of analysis and synthesis, theoretical thinking and probing questions, and problem solving. Intellectually intense children are always searching for the truth. Introspective and planful, they can also be critical and argumentative. The child who is an early reader, who collects toys, who is always asking mature questions about ongoing events from the weather to science to current news events to homelessness has intellectual intensity and overexcitability. Children with this type of intensity can have a photographic memory and an inclination to categorize in detail. Often, these children do well at spelling contests and chess matches because of their intellectual motivation.

For example, when my son Richard was just three years old and his dad was a medical student working at Los Angeles County Hospital, he asked me, "Why do we have to go to the dungeon to have dinner with daddy?" Richard was remembering his favorite Richard Scary storybooks. He saw the hospital where his dad worked as a dungeon similar to the one in a book we read to him every night. Early on, Richard was analyzing and synthesizing ideas. He was eager to study Greek and Latin and to read every book he could find.

Hallmarks of intellectual intensity include:

1. Independent thinking; can analyze and synthesize ideas, concepts about themselves, and the world around them and others
2. Love of solving problems based on ideas that the child is curious about
3. Ability to look underneath the surface of what is observable; psychologically minded

School choice can be traditional if acceleration is an option. These children can do well in early college entrance programs and highly gifted schools. Making sure that intellectually intense children do not become overly shy or withdrawn at school is important.

Imaginational Overexcitability

Children and adults who have imaginational intensity are profoundly interested in sharing their fantasies and the drama in their lives with anyone who will listen. They tell long and complicated stories. Imaginational abilities, which include a vivid sensitivity to the imaginary reality of films, art, electronics, and music, are another form of this type of intensity. This overexcitability can be seen in young children's profound interest in art, drama, costumes, and video games, and their inclination to talk nonstop about their ideas. Older children with this type of overexcitability are interested in creative writing and performing arts. Imaginative children want to understand the meaning of life. Children who have imaginative overexcitability are deeply intense when they express themselves. Or if they are shy, their internal life can be more meaningful to them than their real life. Imaginary friends can become more important than real friends.

Easily imaginative children become bored and daydream in a traditional learning environment. Underachievement is common and hard to turn around. Homework can become a very serious problem. For example, Jonny, a kindergartener I worked with, was so imaginative that he could not concentrate on his schoolwork unless it was interesting for him. Teachers and specialists at a very traditional school thought that he was not smart enough to learn to read. Jon was singled out as a slow student without potential. When Jon's parents moved him to a more progressive school that nurtured his imagination, all academics issues subsided. Jon was able to work up to his potential without any extra support, even in reading and math, which had seemed impossible for him at the traditional private school that he had attended.

Hallmarks of imaginational intensity:

1. When bored, daydreaming to the extent that pretend worlds become real
2. Mixing truth and reality when telling long and complicated stories
3. Vivid recall of dreams and nightmares

Progressive education is most effective for these children who need to be able to access their imagination at school.

Emotional Overexcitability

Emotional intensity with complex feelings, extreme emotions, identification with other people's feelings, and difficulty with transitions are the most common features of this type of overexcitability. An excellent example in young children is separation anxiety that seems extreme in comparison to nongifted children. Older children often show a remarkable maturity in intuitively understanding how other people are thinking and feeling. Emotional overexcitability is a psychological sensibility about motivation in oneself and in others that drives their actions and reactions. Emotionally intense children can understand an everyday interaction as if they were a trained psychologist. Their psychological sensibility is very evident to friends and family.

Emotional intensity motivates children to figure out ways to manipulate their parents and teachers. While their clever behavior can be incredibly amusing, this manipulation can also get a child or teenager in serious trouble they do not foresee. Parents need to keep in mind that judgment lags far behind reasoning in children who are emotionally intense.

Helping these children with transitions is imperative because their intense emotions can eventually lead to or provoke antisocial behavior. For example, emotionally intense children feel their fears so strongly that they cannot sleep alone, or they refuse to go to school. Depression or the opposite, feeling overly responsible for others, is a negative side effect of emotional intensity. Compassion and concern for others is a positive aspect of deep and profound feelings.

Hallmarks of emotional intensity include:

1. Deep empathy and insight into the feelings of others, which can lead to over-reaction or worrying
2. Strong feelings that are often taken too seriously for their age
3. A mixture of feelings all at once that can lead to feeling confused and overwhelmed

School choice depends on accountability in the curriculum. A school that is totally unstructured is not a good choice for an emotionally intense child. Predictability and structure are critical to containing the child's range of intense feelings.

Being able to identify what type of intensity your child demonstrates is very helpful and calming for parents and other teachers and specialists involved in the child's development. The gifted child is no longer seen as just hyperemotional with unusual maturity. Rather, the child is perceived as actually having certain genetic sensitivities and abilities that need to be identified, respected, released, and nurtured. Being able to focus on what is going on with a gifted child and why he or she is so much more challenging than anyone ever imagined he or she can be is incredibly edifying. Parents feel more competent. Grandparents feel a whiff of relief. And teachers, administrators, and specialists have a different perspective on unacceptable behavior such as boredom. When the gifted child's intensities are understood and challenged, he or she will be calmer. In other words, parental advocacy can help direct the child's energy in a positive and understandable way. Bottling up emotions can create despair, emotional fragmentation, and learning issues for these gifted children, who can grow into frustrated adults.

In conclusion, knowledge is power and promotes effective parenting and learning strategies for gifted children and teenagers. When parents, educators, and other specialists know what the problem they are dealing with is related to, solutions are possible. Merely trying random strategies is not necessary. An inaccurate a diagnostic label will be avoided. The gifted student will be given a chance to develop his or her true potential.

STRESS THAT CONTRIBUTES TO OUT OF CONTROL OVEREXCITABILITY

Yes, it is possible to understand what is making your gifted child so high strung and hard to deal with. So after you have calmed yourself and your child down a little, you can start looking for underlying causes of problems in your home life. Here are the most common issues that I have run into as a consultant to parents of gifted children. Addressing these critical issues carefully and with conviction will reduce intensities.

Mismatch between School and Gifted Child

My daughter is having a hard year. She keeps tearing up her drawings and homework. Now, she does not want to get out of bed and go to school. She tells me she does not have any friends to play with at recess or lunch. I wonder if she is being bullied.

—Emily

I have written about the importance of finding the right school for your child and how there is no one size fits all school that will meet the needs of all gifted children. School mismatch can cause serious problems for parents and children, and even for teachers and principals. I know this is true because I have seen the hassles and craziness of mismatch over and over again throughout my career.

When your child is unhappy at school, unable to find friends, bored with schoolwork and homework, or not connecting well with the teacher; high-strung behavior and intensity escalate to nonproductive levels. Of course, continuous intensity based on frustration is a serious problem that needs to be dealt with in the best way that is affordable and practical. Most likely, hoping that your child will get over whatever is bothering him or her is unrealistic and a waste of time. Meeting with the child's teacher and any staff specialists is always the first step. Having an assessment completed, an Individual Educational Plan (IEP) at public schools, or a private evaluation by a psychologist at private schools will show you what might be stressing your child. The evaluation should make specific recommendations for teachers and specialists. All recommendations have to be implemented and evaluated for effectiveness. Staying on top of what the school is doing and expecting changes that will make your child eager to go to school are crucial.

Let's look at some examples.

Brandon was and still is a highly intense child who had difficulty with Mommy and Me classes and preschool. He was an only child who did not want or know how to follow directions. Brandon did what he wanted to do. He would get very upset and throw temper tantrums when he did not get his way. Mom and dad decided to keep him out of preschool to avoid other parents seeing their embarrassing problem. They hoped their son would outgrow his social immaturity and temper tantrums. So when Brandon started kindergarten, he had not been exposed to other children and had a very difficult time engaging with his teacher and classmates. An IEP was requested and completed by the school. Brandon was given the gifted label as well as possible attention deficit disorder or autism spectrum disorder. His classroom behavior did not improve with this school assessment, which included a list of goals for appropriate behavior.

Brandon's parents then decided to send him to another public school that they were told worked well with gifted children. Unfortunately, this large public school was punitive. Brandon got the message that he was a bad child. Brandon's behavior was made worse by the anticipatory anxiety that he felt going to school and then getting in trouble for his behavior. Brandon was asked to leave this new public school, and placement at a school for seriously disturbed children was suggested.

Brandon's parents consulted with me, and I helped them find a small Montessori school that was more nurturing and less rigid. Both parents attended my parenting groups. They were able to gradually learn how to set child-centered limits and to dial down their intensity when they had to discipline Brandon. As the family calmed down and felt less frustrated, Brandon relaxed and was more able to use his words to handle his frustration. Over many months, with the addition of play dates with children from the Montessori school, Brandon was able to go to school and be a productive student who was indeed gifted.

Sally was underachieving at her religious private school. The head of the school asked mom and dad to hold Sally back—to redo kindergarten. Both parents wondered about their daughter's underachievement because she was very quick and creative. Sally was evaluated by a psychologist, who found that indeed she was gifted. The psychologist thought that Sally should be able to complete her school work. Mom and dad consulted with me about school placement. We looked for another school that might have a more individualized and differentiated curriculum. As well, the family was interested in finding teachers who understood Sally's sensitivities. The new progressive developmental school was a much better match for Sally. Expectations were child centered and clear, and follow-through and accountability were stressed. Sally still found it difficult to make friends, even with a great deal of support. With the assistance of a tutor, Sally was able to catch up with her classmates and perform at grade level. Intensity, both emotional and imaginative, continued to make Sally fearful of schoolwork. With ongoing help from psychotherapy and tutoring, Sally learned to work up to her potential and establish some friendships.

John was a shy child who was very tentative about engaging with his schoolwork and school friends. If not encouraged to do otherwise, he liked to play alone at recess and lunch and in day care. As he got older, John was bullied by the more athletic kids at his private school. By second grade, John was reluctant to go to school. The school psychologist evaluated his school phobia as being related to his giftedness. John had a difficult time with friends who were his age. The private school made an effort to work with the students on issues of bullying. The administration suggested that John go to a social skills group. I did not agree with this intervention.

Lindsey, Jon's mother, decided to try to find a therapist who could help Jon feel better about himself. With the help of psychotherapy and additional play dates, John was able to open up to other students, and he began to thrive at school. A move to a different school was not necessary, as it was in the other cases presented earlier in this chapter.

Larry was a high-strung child who had difficulty following school rules. Often, Larry would not go to school. In an attempt to reduce Larry's anxiety and help him find passion at school, his parents moved him from a public to a private religious school. According to Larry's parents, the religious school was not enriching enough for Larry. After two years of fighting with the principal and teachers, Larry's mother worked to get her son admitted to a public school with a gifted component.

Public school was fascinating for this preteen but also emotionally confusing and very overwhelming. Everyone liked Larry and wanted to be his friend. Larry was at a loss socially and could not concentrate at school. He was very anxious over what schoolwork to complete and what friends to connect with. His anxiety and anger turned to rage at his parents, and he was not able to stay at the school. Ongoing psychiatric and psychological help was necessary to help Larry cope with his fear and depression. For over a year, Larry was home schooled. Gradually, with the help of a tutor who was positive and able to challenge and otherwise deal with Larry's giftedness, full-time public school became an option.

All of the children described thus far in this chapter need a particular type of attention to address their unique giftedness. Finding appropriate school placement was critical to their education and emotional well-being. These children were more aware of their unhappiness than their parents and teachers were.

Parenting Disharmony

When parents don't agree on how to parent, children are eager to play one parent off the other parent to get what they want. This common manipulative behavior leads to an ongoing sense of a chaotic family life. Obviously, some shared parental discipline goals and understanding what priorities are important for the child's health and safety are a must. Still, some parents choose to not agree in an attempt to prove their perspective on discipline and child rearing is the "right and best one." Here are some examples of parents working against one another to show that the other parent is wrong and thus enabling their children to regress into childish behavior. Intensity and overexcitability are amplified when families do not agree about what is important.

Lorna and Steve had two children. Their oldest child, Stuart, was an early reader but quite uncomfortable socially. His younger sister, Serena, was socially adept and less sensitive. Stuart was advanced to the highest pre-school class to accommodate his curiosity and reading abilities. Stuart threw temper tantrums after school, and his parents believed it was because kindergarten was so boring for him. Lorna contacted me for help. Did they need a new school? A new house? What would help Stuart be calmer and happier at school and at home? As I got to know the family, it became clear that mom and dad did not agree on parenting. While mom was very talkative and communicative, dad was playful but strict. These differing parenting styles were confusing for Stuart, who was never quiet sure what to expect when he got home from school—easygoing, fun-loving, strict dad or talk about what is going to happen next mom.

Teachers and administrators worked with these parents to provide accel-eration, which was sometimes helpful for Stuart's school adjustment and sometimes a burden for him. I often thought that Stuart was more comfort-able at school than at home. I carefully brought up the effects of their dishar-mony. Lorna and Steve were always certain that doing something would help. Gradually, as a new school and a new house did not provide the happi-ness that Lorna wanted for her children, these parents gained some insight into the negative impact of their disharmonious parenting. Eventually, Stuart told his parents that they confused him and that he was never sure what to expect from his parents. In turn, Stuart's school behavior was very unpredictable. Was Stuart really bored? Or was he just insecure because he got so many mixed messages from his parents? As time went on, I came to understand that parental disharmony was more serious than school placement.

Parents Who Have Disorganized or Confused Priorities

Parents whose own parents were not good role models have a more diffi-cult time getting their priorities straight about how to establish values and set limits. Often in these families, one parent takes the lead, and the other follows. But both parents do not have the deep conviction they need to raise secure gifted children. Disorganized parents give their children too much say about what is important. There are too many choices and not enough conse-quences. Unfocused parents have a hard time working with the school and with specialists because they are not certain enough about what they really want to accomplish as parents. Here are some examples.

Catherine and Kimberley decided to have a child together. Catherine car-ried the child, and Kimberley was the adoptive mother. Both women had come from unhappy home lives and wanted to have a child to love. Cathy had a very difficult birth and suffered from postpartum depression. Kim had very little maternal feeling and limited insight. Kim had difficulty con-necting with her daughter Emily. Both mothers were lost and confused.

Going from specialist to specialist, to parenting groups, and to preschool was very stressful for the whole family. Emily was a high-strung and intense child who demonstrated characteristics of autism spectrum disorder and giftedness. These partners could not agree on what was best for their daughter, who became more and more withdrawn. Issues with socialization are common when gifted children do not get enough positive parenting and appropriate nurturing.

Amanda, who was not married, had a child with a very wealthy man who she thought would support her both financially and emotionally. Their child was highly gifted and emotionally intense. Jared was hard to calm down and suffered from intense separation anxiety from his father, who was more loving and playful than his mother. Jared's care was often relegated to nannies and grandparents. While there was enough of everything to go around, Amanda and Tony could not agree on anything. Since Amanda was very determined, she was able to get her way, even if what she wanted was not good for Jared. Teachers, administrators, and specialists worked hard to educate these parents. And they are still trying. Emotional intensity and separation anxiety are present and very disturbing when Jared senses his mom or dad is angry or unavailable.

Miranda, a beautiful and talented actress, was married to a Broadway producer named Bill. Miranda was unable to calm down Harriett, her gifted child. Miranda, a graduate of an Ivy League school, read every book on child rearing. Miranda gave her husband summaries of what she had learned in her research on how to parent. Parenting groups and baby classes, and then Mommy and Me and preschool, were chosen with care. Bill showed Harriett how to swim laps. At one year, she could do five laps in the family pool. Obviously, she had psychomotor overexcitability.

No one, including grandparents and nannies, seemed to be able to calm Harriett down. Her emotional intensity was something to be reckoned with. The solution to the problem of containing Harriett's intensity seemed to be to choose one approach to parent and follow through, but Miranda could never decide what approach she consistently wanted to take. Her husband Bill was too busy to really concern himself with his daughter.

These parents who did not have parents who were adequate role models are confused about the best way to parent. In their quest to be the "best" parents and redo their own childhoods, they give their children way too much power and authority. Serious complications arise because gifted children can sense when their parents are not sure of themselves. Gifted kids can react manipulatively from an early age when they receive too many mixed messages from insecure parents. They can act out their intensity and overexcitability in destructive and confusing behaviors that are very hard for parents and teachers to understand.

Parents with Financial and Child Care Issues

Parents can want everything for their children and sacrifice way too much of their money and energy for extras they cannot afford. Choosing a private school when you can't afford one creates serious problems for the entire family. It is very possible to raise gifted kids on a budget. If both parents have to go back to work, child care can become an ongoing problem that makes children anxious and intensely unhappy. There is continuous pressure on parents and children related to schedules, school meetings, and getting homework completed. Having established and effective child care is critical. Valuing the time you spend with your child is priceless. Children feel ignored when there is too much stress in the family over day-to-day issues and there is not enough time to develop the child's potential. Here is an example of how harried parents create problems for their precocious kids.

Essie and Rinaldo had their children later in life. Although their ethnic backgrounds were very unique, both parents came from emotionally negligent and abusive families. Comfortable enough financially without children, they did not realize the cost and stress of raising two children. They bought a home in an expensive neighborhood with a top-rated school district. Both were certain that they had made the right decision about the right neighborhood school and that all of their schooling problems were solved. Both parents were totally shocked when their oldest son, Sam, started having "boredom" issues at school. These problems were more profound because Sam was imaginatively intense and easily bored at school.

Unfortunately, the economy crashed, and this highly competitive school was not geared toward gifted children. Parents at this school were uptight and unkind. The stress of the wrong school and a lack of resources due to unemployment created so much stress for the two children that eventually both were diagnosed with depression. Social and school phobia along with underachievement were issues these parents had to contend with on a shoestring budget. Changing Sam's school was helpful, but a great deal of damage had already been done. Helping Sam catch up with his peers was difficult. Underachievement became a serious issue.

While this story may sound drastic, it is very common today. Getting in over one's head financially can create family stress that gifted children take seriously and to heart. When intense and sensitive children feel like they are a burden and that their life is not stable and predictable, they begin to feel overwhelmed. Some children act out with behavior problems such as not doing homework. Blaming themselves as well, they can withdraw into sadness and hopelessness to avoid further anxiety.

Overparenting

Examples of overidentification are present throughout this book, and some general wisdom can be gleaned. Simply stated, micromanaging parents who know what they want and when they want it can make themselves "crazy" and their children enraged and insecure. People who overparent raise children who lack resilience and the motivation to succeed without the help of mom, dad, or nanny. And of course, there is a fine line between being caring and being overbearing. Here is a positive example.

Judy, a mother who emotionally mothered her mother, wanted to give her children what she dad not gotten. Her life revolved around her children's needs for attention, play dates, and intellectual stimulation. Play groups, and then schools, were always supported to the maximum. Judy had a script to follow. Stay home with the kids, work at the children's schools, and spend family time with all of the grandparents. Frequent visits from grandparents made her crazy, but she hosted them anyway. Incidentally, the overload of love also made her children feel anxious, entitled, helpless, and fearful. Judy wore her heart on her shoulder for her gifted kids. Because the indulgent attention Judy gave was so authentic, it was easier to help her children become more independent as they grew up, but. it was a long road that we travelled helping Judy learn that too much was really too much.

Parental Indifference

Fathers often leave the decision making to mom. Or some mothers who have stay at home husbands leave the decision making to dad. The worst case scenario is when the nanny and specialists are left to make the serious decisions about child care and education. Unfortunately, when this type of parenting arrangement is all that is available, gifted children learn to manipulate their caregivers to their advantage.·

Sometimes, having dad in the background can be a relief because there is no turmoil in the house over who is right and who is wrong. Unfortunately, the parent in charge does not have enough me time. Parents who have no help and run from one stressful situation to the next have limited resources for child rearing. When one parent is always on the parenting treadmill, children gain too much power.

Divorce

Thoughtful parents can and do get divorced, and this decision can be in the children's best interests. However, a family that cannot agree how to manage the family under one roof usually does not have a calm and well-staged divorce. Anger and resentments can trickle down to sensitive and high-strung children, who blame themselves for marital unhappiness and act out their own anger and insecurity at home and at school. Psycho-therapeutic support and insight can be indicated if children fall behind at school or are unhappy and withdrawn. Children of divorce can be very angry that their well-established life is changing, which only exacerbates their normal intensity. Regaining a stable home situation is critical and needs to be a priority for parents, who often fail to focus on the children's issues.

CONCLUSIONS

Ways to Calm Your Child and Yourself Down in the Face of an Intensity Storm

1. *First things first.* The parent needs to be calm before he or she can calm the child down. So always keep this in mind when you are upset, overwhelmed, screaming, or crying about what went wrong. You are upsetting your child. Know that your out-of-control upset is making the already dreadful situation worse and intensifying your child's fears. Because emotional intensity is a characteristic of gifted children, try to put your upset into perspective by planning for intensity outburst events. Accept that you have to deal with your child's sensitivity, even though you wish you didn't. There are no easy solutions.
2. *Remember you are the boss.* If you are the boss, then negotiating is your decision, not your child's decision. Listen carefully. Acknowledge your child's feelings. Calmly decide if you want to take what your child has to say seriously. Sometimes, gifted children can spin the mistakes they make into fabulous arguments that are totally beside the point of the issue at hand.
3. *Be clear about the family rules,* which should be child centered but not child driven. If your children understand what you expect, they will have a harder time wiggling out of the consequences that they rightly deserve for breaking a rule. Emotional intensities are easier to deal with if the child knows that you have his or her best interest at heart. Irrational out of context limits and consequences enrage and exaggerate intensities.
4. *Avoid long speeches* about why you have made a decision, as this effectively gives up your power. When you ramble on about why you are doing something, which most likely you have previously gone over, your message loses its power and authority. Remember that you are the boss and don't need to explain your rules that have already been clearly delineated.
5. *Establish your credibility and hold on to it.* Try to get the point across that you are smarter than your child because of your experiences in life. Gifted kids lack judgment, but they are remarkable at reasoning. Teach them to respect your wisdom. This lesson of respect will serve your family well as your children grow into teenagers and adults.
6. If you *find enticing motivators* to help your child follow the rules, the rules become fun to follow and achieve. Building bridges to accomplishment through follow-through is very important in our competitive world.

7. *Have some realistic short-term consequences* that help set limits but do not make your child feel totally humiliated.
8. *Use praise and positive reinforcement* to encourage your child to keep on trying. Avoid being negative.
9. *Find a support group* of friends and relatives who can listen to you and not be critical or demeaning of your parenting problems.
10. To show them that you can be a participant in their games or adventures, *let your children make up some of the rules* that have to be followed.
11. *Avoid doing what does not work for you and your family,* even if an important advisor strongly suggests doing so. What works for one child may not work for another.
12. *Make your own life important* so that you do not encourage your child's demanding behavior. A family should be a cooperative unit of people working together.

5

Gifted Children's Common Learning Struggles

Olivia wants to be perfect in every way. I think she feels that she has to be and that if she had to ask for help or ask for clarification or permission, it would essentially "out" her as not being perfect. I think she has always been this way—she was born with this trait. I recognize it in her because I feel I am a perfectionist. It scares me because I know that my own sense of perfectionism keeps me [even now] from even starting something because if I am not assured that it will be perfect, I am paralyzed and cannot even begin.

—Helene

THE MYTH OF THE RIGHT SCHOOL

Gifted children have unique learning problems based on their perfectionism, quick thinking, and asynchronous development. Out of control emotional intensity, boredom, distraction, procrastination, disorganization, and executive functioning issues are outgrowths or side effects of their unique cognitive and emotional learning style. Driven parents, perfectionistic parents, single and divorced parents, busy and overwhelmed parents, and even indifferent parents naively believe that if they can just find the right school, their bright and intense child will be easy to educate. This parental logic is based on a lack of understanding the real but often unspoken learning struggles of gifted children, and it leads parents into believing the Right School Myth, which is a serious parenting trap.[1] Every child is unique, and every family situation related to schooling has its own strengths and limitations. Parents need to find a school that works with their individual needs, financial situation, and emotional assets and concerns.

The reality of educating a gifted child is far, far more complicated than meets the eye. Finding a school that is prepared to challenge your child's learning highs and lows, boredom, and social anxiety has to understand and be prepared to value diversity in learning styles and progressive philosophies of how children learn. Perfectionism will lead gifted children to overachievement or procrastination and underachievement. Managing your child's learning struggles is hard but manageable if you try to take baby steps and have discrete attainable goals. Patience, persistence, and staying on track to achieve minigoals are also helpful because they model for your child the way to approach a problem with learning. Pressuring children with a frantic do or die intensity to achieve or ignoring their problems is very counterproductive, as it undermines their ability to develop problem-solving strategies. Here are two examples of how parents have worked with the school environment or have ignored problems a child is confronting in the hope that the school could handle the problems.

Let It Be Parenting

Barbara's mother Irene called me to help her get her 14-year-old daughter organized. Barbara was having difficulty completing her homework. Irene and Joe wanted their daughter to raise her B's to A's. Mom reported that Barbara had been identified in first grade as gifted. The family lived in a very prestigious school district that had honors and gifted programs, and Barbara could walk to her elementary school. In elementary school, she was shy about making friends and participating in social activities. In addition, Barbara's expectations for other children were unrealistic because her school friends did not interact like adults did. Still, Barbara was always at the top of her class academically.

In middle school, Barbara continued to keep to herself. However, she began to struggle to complete her work. Once she reached high school, her problems with homework, time management, and organization became increasingly serious obstacles to good grades. Barbara had very few friends because she was awkward and undersocialized. Both parents were concerned that Barbara would have trouble throughout high school and with getting into college because of her disorganization, procrastination, and social issues.

The learning problem Barbara had in the classroom started early in life. Her parents, Irene and Ted, spoke with specialists who said that perhaps Barbara's had a tendency toward Asperger syndrome. After that provisional diagnosis, no further interventions were considered. Was Barbara really fine on her own until middle school, when she had more homework and felt more pressure to fit in? Her parents continued to ignore Barbara's issues with learning how to learn at school. Barbara became very isolated from other students.

In high school, Irene and Ted began to pressure their daughter to work harder. They wanted me to teach her study skills, which they thought were a "quick fix." Unfortunately, Barbara's school problems had been going on for far too long. They were too deep rooted to respond to a simple behavioral solution. A great deal of talk therapy and directed social skills interventions were indicated. Irene and Joe had difficulty putting faith in this more labor-intensive approach. They chose to continue to look for study skills coaching and to ignore the issues of asynchronicity that had led to Barbara's underachievement.

A Proactive Approach

Gary and Robin knew that their child was gifted because of his deep curiosity, very advanced verbal skills, and emotional intensity. Nathan was evaluated by a private psychological consultant who informed them that Nathan had an IQ in the 99th percentile. Nathan also demonstrated learning highs and lows. Unlike Irene and Ted, these parents took their son's learning issues, coupled with his perfectionism, seriously. Proactive in their approach to parenting, they consulted with many different specialists and read and attended meetings about gifted children. They carefully looked at school options. They selected a school that was academically focused but also nurturing to help their son develop confidence.

Nathan was very verbal but also shy and sensitive. He would cry easily at school if he did not get the right answer. Math was a particular problem, and a tutor was hired to help Nathan gain self-confidence. Along the way, these parents modeled problem solving in their own lives and helped Nathan cope with his struggles. They spoke with Nathan about friendships and disappointments. Pressure to achieve was absent from their vision of how to be good parents. Nathan wanted to do well at school because he was interested. While Nathan's perfectionism never disappeared, procrastination was not a problem either.

Parents Who Are Attentive and Proactive Make a Dierence

The difference in parenting styles, a proactive approach rather than a live and let live approach, was critical to neutralizing asynchronous development for Nathan. By being attentive and solving problems related to learning highs and lows as they came up, Nathan's parents were able to help their son develop his potential. In sharp contrast, Barbara's parents believed that because she was gifted, she would learn on her own. They fell into some of the most common parenting traps (see Chapter 7). Consequently, they had more serious issues to deal with when their daughter began to underachieve because of the entanglements between perfectionism, procrastination, and a lack of persistence. Most of Barbara's problems were related to underdeveloped social skills and organization issues, which definitely led her to avoid other students and to procrastinate in the agenda for success she created for herself. Breaking this pattern was a serious struggle, even though school placement was more than adequate.

PERFECTIONISM INHIBITS AND UNDERMINES PERSISTENCE

When parents believe they can get around the issue of how perfectionism undermines persistence, they are on the wrong road. There are no easy answers when it comes to school choice. There is no one size fits all school. Parents need to educate themselves about how to parent in relation to their child's perfectionistic behavior. Parents often ask, "What is the root of my child's learning struggles?" This is a question that teachers, specialists, and parents have to consider if they are going to have any success working with asynchronicity, that is, the ups and downs of the gifted child's behavior.

While there is no one explanation for perfectionistic tendencies in gifted children, my experiences lead me to believe the following. Perfectionism and an instantaneous need to take charge of an activity are why learning struggles and school issues develop. The precocious child is very alert and curious, and he or she wants and needs to connect with caregivers, activities, and early stimulation intensely. Naturally (or at least we hope this is a natural reaction), parents react to their child's intensity by trying to soothe their child. The child develops an attachment with his or her mother and other caregivers that is based on intensity. Because attachment is based on immediacy, the child's perfectionism is inadvertently reinforced and perpetuated. The bond between child and parents promotes the gifted child's innate perfectionism. Overexcitability, including emotional intensity, confounds their passion and persistence, or their procrastination (see Chapter 4).

Observable very early in life, perfectionism, passion, and persistence are dominant personality traits that direct the gifted child's behavior. When the capacity for concentrating on passionate interests is positively fueled—motivated by intense curiosity—gifted children will be able to follow a life path that allows them to develop their unique potential. Unfortunately, intense curiosity can be stifled when perfectionism derails persistence and motivation. This type of inhibition narrows a child's initiative, interests, and interactions with other children, parents, and teachers. Perfectionism can seriously limit or arrest development of the whole child's potential. The earlier the dynamic between perfectionism and lack of persistence is acknowledged, delineated, and understood by parents, the less likely this force of nature will undermine the gifted child's development. Further, by understanding the roots of their child's perfectionism through an assessment of overexcitability, parents can become better teachers and advocates for their child.

Persistence predicts success and fulfillment in gifted children. Parenting that develops persistence is critical and can be extremely challenging with perfectionistic children. Easily, persistence, passion, and perfectionism can become tangled up in a gridlock of inaction that leads to avoidance of difficult tasks and underachievement. Untangling this gridlock can be difficult and confusing. Avoiding perfectionistic entanglements is critical. How parents manage their child's perfectionism seems to be the most important key to dealing with the tendency for gifted children to overfocus, limit their horizons, or avoid difficult tasks. Acknowledgement of the tendency to have difficulty with transitions, stopping a project that is not finished perfectly, is the first step toward conquering this problem behavior. Ignoring procrastination or denying that it is a problem is a recipe for developing counterproductive long-standing achievement issues. Escalating the difficulty your child has with changes will make the problem more intense.

When you see that your child resists stopping what he/she is supposed to stop doing, take a calm but firm stance, as this will help diffuse your child's intensity related to having to listen to your directions. You could say, "Now it is time to go on to the next project of the morning. You can go back to working on your Legos later this afternoon. I can see how much you enjoy building Legos." Empathizing with your child's anxiety, fear, anger, or frustration is extremely helpful because he or she will feel understood. As you set limits on what expectations or behaviors are appropriate in a particular situation, your child will become a better listener. When your child is calm, talk the problem through and help your child use his or her own words to summarize the problematic behavior or fear. To summarize, here are some strategies that may be useful in reducing procrastination.

Strategies to Reduce Procrastination

1. Accept that you are in charge of your support team. Create a great team that works together effectively by evaluating and re-evaluating goals for your child and family.
2. Understand that transitions are hard for gifted perfectionistic children and give them warning about a possible change in activity.
3. Keep in mind that not being able to transition or not listening (a form of procrastination) is directly related to perfectionism. Do not ignore your child's issues with listening and following rules.
4. On the other hand, be child centered. Stay off your high horse. Do not escalate your child's struggles because pressure makes them more intense and ashamed.

Perfectionism is sure to come into play, and then their problem seems much worse to everyone than it was to start with.Maintain a strong, calm, and positive attitude about how you can and will help your child.

5. Remember that you are right about your child having to follow the rules. Your child will not necessarily agree with you. Gifted children are brilliant negotiators. You are in charge.

6. Empathize with their feelings to let them know that you understand how hard a time they are having with the responsibilities they need to fulfill.

7. Set limits with consequences when your child does not present work that demonstrates that he or she is accountable.

Here are some thoughts that the mothers I work with in parenting group shared about dealing with their children's perfectionism.

Carolyn says, *Daniela can be perfectionistic to the point where it paralyzes her. She won't try something because she is afraid she won't do it correctly the first time. An example of this happened during piano lesson and she refused to play a new piece of music for her teacher. Her teacher told her she had to stop and leave the lesson if she didn't try. She chose to leave instead of try.*

Fortunately, Daniela's mother talked with her daughter and the teacher to make a plan for the next lesson, which has already been paid for. Hopefully, Danny will adjust to her new teacher, who she says "talks to her like a baby." The decision to change teachers has not been made. Mom is waiting to see how her daughter responds in the next couple of lessons.

Julie says, *My child will sometimes not attempt an activity unless he knows he will be the best. Adam won't even try if he cannot be the best. If he does something that is not good or needs work, he will make an excuse as to why he was not the best. He will say "Oh, I'm sick,'" or "Oh, my legs hurts."*

Julie knows that her son Adam uses excuses because he is a perfectionist. While she empathizes with his fears, she does not let him give up on trying. She uses positive reinforcement when he is successful to encourage his new behaviors. Julie talks to Adam about how everything he does is not going to be done perfectly, especially the first time. Julie gives examples from her own life about the struggles she had with learning a new behavior.

Rebecca says, *My son, Dylan, is reluctant to try activities if he isn't invested in them. He loves reading and hates sports. I always wonder if this because he is worried he isn't good at sports or he really isn't interested? Perfectionism turns into underachieving and a lot of quitting when something is boring or hard.*

Rebecca is very attuned to her child's often manipulative reactions. Like Julie, she focuses on getting him to try the activities that he says he hates. Whether she discusses or negotiates, Rebecca is always tuned into the problem and looking for a solution that makes Dylan feel better about himself. She does not give into his perfectionism. On the other hand, she is careful not to pressure him or ignore his feelings.

PARENTING STRATEGIES THAT ARE HELPFUL IN TAMING PERFECTIONISM

Effective parents are very aware that perfectionist behavior is normal and based on fear. They understand the importance of redirection. They don't give into their children's demands or ignore their feelings. Trying to normalize a child's frustration is the most useful first step as it reduces any feelings of shame. Putting whatever the issue is into perspective for the child reduces stress for everyone. You might say, "I can help you solve the problem because I had this same problem when I was your age." Or you could try saying, "I was very afraid to go to school and wanted to stay home. My mom stayed longer in my classroom for three days, and that helped." Or give your child other solutions to their problems. For example, for a shy child, you might say, "I used to be afraid to talk up in class, but I practiced a little bit with my dad, and that really helped me speak up. Should we try this as a strategy?" Talk about the details of the problem with hands-on solutions and show your child the baby steps of progress he or she is making.

What *not* to do is easy to say. Follow-through requires containing your own fears. Do not make the problem worse than it actually is. In other words, don't cry over spilled milk because it sets you up as a bad role model for your child. Don't demand that your child shape up or ship out, as this is unrealistic and something said in anger. If you model sensible reactions, you will show your child how to be a mature person.

Always try to normalize your child's behavior problems by giving examples of how you and other families and children have the same or similar struggles. For example, last week I told Henry, a gifted child, that 97 out of 100 gifted kids that I know do not like sports. This fact really helped Henry put his problem into perspective. He agreed to go to baseball practice and try his hardest, even if he was not the best person on his team.

WHAT IS ASYNCHRONOUS DEVELOPMENT?

Asynchronous development—uneven abilities or learning highs and lows—defines giftedness, according to phenomenological psychologists. If you have a gifted child, she or he will have asynchronous development— high abilities and lower abilities.[2] The discrepancy in learning abilities creates confusion about how to master what does not come immediately. Because quick thinking is the rule for gifted kids, they become self-conscious and unsure about how to proceed when they need to learn something. Remember, they are very quick learners and may not know *how* to learn, that is, how to walk themselves through the learning process. Precocious children face learning encounters at school without having strategies for problem solving.

They give up on a task if they don't know how to do it immediately. Helping your child deal with nonimmediate answer retrieval can be the biggest challenge you face in educating him or her. Incidentally, the brighter the child, the greater the span of learning abilities, a situation that gets worse as the child becomes older. Eventually, avoidant behavior becomes a defensive strategy for not completing their work. Unfortunately, the child falls farther and farther behind and will have a great deal of difficulty catching up, even if he or she is gifted. For example, Lizzy may be reluctant to learn reading because her brother was such a good reader without any effort. Lizzy decides it is too hard for her to learn to read. She has to learn how to learn to read and needs to be taught how to persist when she needs to struggle.

Parents call me with two common questions related to asynchronous development. First, parents often ask, "Why does my son have all of the behavioral characteristics of a gifted child and yet he is not able to read?" Another recurring question is, "Why does my daughter, who is a strong reader, have so much difficulty going to school and playing with the other children?"

My answer to parents' questions is, "Asynchronous development." Maturity and ability levels between an exceptional talent and social skills overlap at different rates and create learning problems that easily become fixed in place by the tidal wave of perfectionism. Here are two examples of common problems that gifted children experience.

Aidan, who is seven, is able to understand the abstract and intellectual issues of a ten-year-old. Emotionally, his maturity level is that of a five-year-old. The span between ten years and five years creates frustration for Aidan, his parents, and his teachers. He gets easily discouraged and wants to run away from his classroom. He gets agitated and acts out his anger with other children on the playground by hitting and kicking. Aidan prefers to stay home to avoid the frustration of getting in trouble for his misbehavior. Teachers do not know how to contain Aidan's anger. He is continually in the principal's office. Once the school paired Aidan with an understanding teacher with a small classroom, he slowly calmed down.

Marcy is only eight years old, but she is able to read at a high school level. Her art projects are detailed and imaginative. She loves math. However, Marcy has a hard time going to school, as she misses her mother's attention. She has difficulty making friends and tends to rely on her older brother for help in social situations. Marcy chooses to stay in the library during recess and lunch. Teachers and administration have a hard time helping Marcy engage in social activities. Special play dates and psychotherapy helps Marcy interact with others at school.

Keep in mind that both highs and lows are worthy of your attention. Let your child know you can help, no matter what the issue. Be positive about teaching your child to solve his or her learning challenges, as he or she will give up if you give up. Pointing out progress is always helpful when a gifted child feels inadequate and helpless.

PROCRASTINATION—A CRY FOR HELP

I hear stories all the time from parents about how hard it is to get their young children's teeth brushed and to get them into bed. The reading ritual can get out of control, and your "darling" child can manipulate you into staying in his or her room just a little bit longer. This behavior is the forerunner to avoidant behavior and procrastination. Actually, procrastination is a red flag that the gifted child is having emotional issues with perfectionism, schoolwork, or whatever else he or she is avoiding, such as fitting in socially. The longer the problem with avoidance lasts and the more embedded it becomes, the more serious an issue it can be for the child's education and emotional well-being. In addition, social and school frustration can lead to despair and clinical depression.[3]

Procrastination, a defense against narcissistic injury, is the child's way of protecting himself or herself from feeling incomplete or damaged—imperfect. While this defensive behavioral strategy is not necessarily a conscious decision, the behavior is carried implemented with great vigor and determination. This incredibly frustrating behavior, which is based on anxiety and fear, looks different in different children and in different situations. Here are some patterns of procrastination that I have heard of while consulting with parents of gifted children. Some children manifest one or two forms of procrastination. Others, at one time or another, manifest all forms of procrastination.

The Fearful Child

While all gifted children are highly sensitive to separation from their families, it is more difficult for the fearful child to get involved with other children and new environments. These children are emotionally intense and easily overexcitable. Both boys and girls can have deep fears that keep them from being developmentally independent in social situations. Their extreme attachment to their parents and siblings keeps them from developing appropriate social skills. It is hard to know when their fearfulness becomes avoidance and procrastination. Eventually, fear does lead to procrastination, which is a difficult problem to solve.

Jackie says, *Emmy has always stuck by my side no matter where we go. At the park, at school, at her grandparent's house, she clings to me. I don't know what to do.*

Anita says, *Marty is afraid to go anywhere without me. He likes hanging out with his sister and grandparents. Yesterday when we were at the toy store, we saw one of his friends from school. Marty was terrified to even say hello. He ran to hide behind me. I had to stay with him at preschool longer than the other mothers stayed with their children.*

Helene says, *Olivia relies on her brother to do her talking for her, and she is in third grade now. I am afraid to separate them. I know it is not good for my son to take care of Olivia, who needs to learn to speak up.*

Obviously, helping fearful gifted children to be more confident is extremely important to their development, both academically and socially. But fearful children present unique problems that are best dealt with in school settings, where teachers and administrators are knowledgeable about how to bring out natural talent and initiative. With children who are fearful, I always recommend a progressive and developmental school, as these non-traditional schools individualize their curriculum to meet the unique learning challenges of their students. Rigid expectations found at traditional schools are not emphasized. The fearful child's self-esteem is enhanced, not thwarted.

When fearfulness intrudes on schooling, psychological interventions such as parent coaching and psychotherapy may be necessary. But parents also need to help their children over come their fears. Parents should talk with their children about why they are anxious about being with other children and then make a plan for positive social experiences. Sometimes, social experiences will be successful; sometimes, they will not work out. Acknowledging the child's social awkwardness or uncertainty is what is important. It is also critical to continually attempt to overcome the problem by helping the child make and enjoy friends. When parents negatively evaluate the child's social progress, social emotional growth is stifled. It is best to always try and find a positive aspect of a social experience. For example, parents might say, "I am so proud of you for taking the opportunity to introduce yourself to your new friends." This attitude encourages social growth, while showing disappointment in outcomes decreases the child's motivation to try.

The "I Can't Do It" Child

Different from the fearful child who has a quiet temperament,[4] this is the gifted kid who has learned to be helpless because his or her mother and father overidentify with their child's struggles. Parents and children in these types of relationships are emotionally intense. What is different is that these parents confuse their issues with their child's issues and let their child get away with being lazy and giving up. They tend to be over-reactive, overprotective, and performance product orientated.

Donna says, *Pablo likes me to help him with his schoolwork. He won't do any work on his own without some support from a tutor or teacher.*

He is falling behind, even though he is extremely bright and capable of working on his own. The teacher thinks Pablo is lazy and that I am not involved enough in his day-to-day care. I have to work, and I have a great nanny.

Alison says, *Matthew feels helpless in new situations. And he has to be sure that other children will play with him before we leave him for a play date. Sometimes, he is so bossy and demanding that other children don't want to follow his rules of playing. We keep trying to encourage play dates.*

These mothers have realized, a little too late, that they need to have more realistic expectations for their children. These parents will need the support of teachers and therapists to help their children want to learn to be independent. Learned helplessness is different from fear because it is based on an established pattern of thought, which is more difficult to diffuse.

The "Uber" Independent Child

The uber-independent child is introverted and careful. Intellectual over-excitability and intensity are hallmarks of the uber independent child's way of reacting to their world. These are children who have very few friends and can be very comfortable playing in the corner or on the sidelines. It is not unusual for this type of child to get overwhelmed when they are in large groups. Because they can be sensitive to what others expect, they keep to themselves, even with adults. Jeannie shares her daughter's issues, which are very similar to other uber-independent gifted kids.

Perfectionism and procrastination manifest in our daughter as anxiety. There is never enough time. And no matter the content, the result is never what she could really do. If she has four weeks to create a writing assignment, she will wait till the last days. She says she is allowing the formulation in her mind to grow and that not a word can be typed until it is fully formed. There is always stress around the first printout. There has never been enough time to fully execute what she has imagined in its perfect and proper form.

Alison says, *Leslie has to get the answer on her own. We try to help with her schoolwork and even with cleaning up her bedroom, but she refuses to let us help her. No matter how anxious she is about what needs to be done, she knows that she is always the best at everything and that no one can help her.*

The stubbornness of the uber-independent gifted child is really hard to deal with, no matter what secret strategies you employ or what enlightened experts you consult. Driven and persistent in their inability to listen to others, their intense stubbornness is based on an unshakeable belief that they are right about everything. Know-it-all behavior is so compelling that the uber-independent gifted child is hard to reason with. Often, these smart kids get into trouble with authority figures. While defiance is not the root of their problem, gradually, if this type of grandiosity is not dealt with at school and at home, it does turn into defiance and anti-social behavior.

Setting limits and following through with consequences for not getting work completed is essential. Discussing, explaining, and even labeling the procrastination and stubbornness is also a good way to reduce their uncertainty in themselves. You could say, "I know that you are procrastinating about cleaning up your room. Can you tell me what feels so hard about getting your stuff organized?"

The Dreamer

Dreamers are happy to make up personal solutions to projects they develop on their own based on imagination and creativity. Imaginative intensity and overexcitability drive these children's actions and reactions. Dreamers have difficulty getting their work completed on time or at all. Procrastination is entangled with intense curiosity. However, dreamers are not as defiant as the uber-independent child. Reasoning with them can help dreamers become more based in reality.

John says, *My son Alan has perfect ideas—wild, creative ideas about how he would like to conceive a project. He can spend all of his time thinking, dreaming, and planning. None of his time is spent doing the project. In the end, he has no time to implement any of his ideas, or very few, because he spent so much time thinking about what he wanted to do.*

Kevin says, *My daughter, three-year-old Eleanor, is interested in black holes, and that is all she wants to talk about. Elli dreams she will become an astronaut and go into outer space someday.*

Dreamers need to learn how to spend "time on task" so that they can learn basics at school and develop their potential. Finding a school that allows for diversity and creativity is critical. With the right school, setting up a predictable structure for these children is usually enough to get them to do their schoolwork. It is necessary to ensure they stay on task. Letting a problem with dreaming get out of control easily leads to underachievement and even school failure.

The Critic

Critics are critical of what is given to them to work on at home or at school. They don't want to do their homework because it is "dumb," "not interesting," or "boring." Intellectually intense and capable of being manipulative, these children prefer video games and other electronics. Critics are single-minded in their disdain for what they call stupidity, and parents find it difficult to motivate them to do simple tasks and just get them out of the way. This form of procrastination can infuriate parents and teachers alike. Consequences are necessary to get this behavior under control. When this behavior dominates, family life is a serious struggle.

Brigette says, *Jenny likes to procrastinate on schoolwork that she feels is a waste of her time. She says that the work is too easy, and she would rather be doing something else.*

Betty says, *Scarlett often feels insulted or offended by how easy her homework is, and easy homework makes her procrastinate. She would rather sit down and stare into space than do homework that she considers boring.*

Henry says, *Nico wants to explore and research animals. He can spend hours on the computer and never look at his easy homework. The teacher thinks we are not strict enough, but she does not understand how bad and intense he can be.*

Procrastination based on criticism of the work that needs to be done can be confusing to parents and teachers. Some parents agree with their child without thinking about how much power they are giving away. Critics make themselves authorities on what needs to be done. At the same time, they try to get out of doing what they fear they are not good at. There can be a great deal of confusion, manipulation, and overidentification in this type of procrastination. Parents need to sort out what is really going on underneath the confusion their child is creating. Parent coaching and psychological evaluations are useful in getting children to accept that they have to do their schoolwork, even if they think it is boring and stupid.

The Troublemaker

"Is my child deaf?" This type of child is a negative attention seeker. Most of the time, the troublemaker has felt ignored by his or her parents. And this parental question ("Is my child deaf?") usually indicates a child who gets his or her own way by directly ignoring and enraging his or her parents. Troublemakers are emotionally intense and manipulative. I have never met a child who does not listen who is seeking negative attention. This subtle type of manipulation is not mean spirited. It is based on an emotional intensity that is sensitive to rejection. It is actually a way of getting negative attention from mom and dad, which seems better than just being ignored. Once this negative pattern of getting his or her own way begins to work for the child, the pattern is hard to stop. Seekers of negative attention have difficulty with teachers and friends. Most likely, they are not getting the love they need at home.

Julie says, *Angelina and I had a huge fight, and Angie started swearing and screaming. In frustration, I took a washcloth and washed my daughter's mouth out with soap.*

Jonathan says, *Daisy does not like to eat dinner at the dinner table. Every night, she makes a scene and is sent to her room. In her room alone, she will tear up all of her homework and then come out and scream at her mother and me.*

Fred says, *Sadie said that she could not sleep alone in her own bed. We tried everything but locking her door. Every night, she would end up sleeping in our bedroom. This went on for years until she was sent away to sleep away camp, where she learned to sleep without us.*

Children who use angry behavior to get their way usually feel unworthy of their parents' love because they have been ignored. Psychotherapy to deal with issues of self-esteem is usually necessary to diminish this behavior. Family therapy is also helpful, as it helps strengthen the attachment between parent and child. School phobias and refusal to sleep alone are difficult issues to resolve quickly in psychotherapy. But the problem can be resolved with the help of a professional who can understand your gifted child.

Attention Seekers

This type of child's procrastination is hard to figure out when it first starts; it is a way of self-expression. These imaginatively intense children figure out that attention seeking—looking for attention in dramatic and creative ways—is extremely rewarding. Their "show-off" behavior can alienate peers and teachers. Parents may be more entertained by their child's dramatic and creative adventures but gradually tire of them and see them as a way of changing direction from what needs to be accomplished.

Erin says, *Paul knew that he would get attention from his father if he wrote a story that was part of his homework for next week. Paul loves to write out and tell stories that are long and detailed. As a way of getting attention, he wrote up a pretend assignment to get his father's attention. The teacher did not accept the story as part of the homework assignment.*

Brenda says, *Dotty likes to procrastinate so that she gets attention from us. She does not like to make choices about what she wants to wear or will try on multiple outfits. The decision about what to wear goes on and on, and she is only four. Dotty knows that we will intervene and help her pick out her clothes and get dressed, even though she is capable of doing this herself. For some reason, she seems to need extra attention at the wrong time.*

Attention seekers have parents who are indecisive about what in is their child's best interest. They see their children's creativity and high energy as positive. Often, they reinforce dramatic behavior or creativity when such behavior is inappropriate. These well-meaning parents have difficulty limiting their expectations because they are smart and tend to overthink available options. Being pragmatic about what is and is not important is very helpful; it is also very difficult to implement. The support of teachers, therapists, and tutors is necessary to redirect this grandiose behavior.

In conclusion, procrastination can be seen in different behavioral problems. Parents have told me that their children have more than one style of procrastination. I am sure that gifted kids are smart enough to try different methods to get their way. Determining how to turn your child's undermining behavior around can be extremely difficult. If you need the help of a tutor or mental health professional, do not hesitate to get advice and support. Proactive behavior, structured problem solving, and measuring success will help diminish and eventually solve your child's problems with procrastination. Always keep in mind that you have a difficult task that takes time and persistence to get under control.

DEVELOPING PERSISTENCE AND DEFEATING THE ENEMIES: PERFECTIONISM AND PROCRASTINATION

Breaking my ideas down into smaller pieces will help you redirect your gifted child's problematic behavior. When you are calm, your child will be able to listen to you. He or she will be more likely to complete responsibilities. When you are frustrated and seem out of control, your child will withdraw to avoidant and perfectionist behavior. You are the force that will teach your child to be persistent. To help you help your procrastinating child, imagine that you are stuck in a horrendous traffic jam, and your frustration level is at ten on a scale of one to ten. Here are rules you need to follow to get safely out of the traffic jam, that is, they will help you deal with your challenging child's unbearable procrastination and perfectionist behavior.

Rule One: Accept Your Child's Intensity.
Perfectionism is part of the child's personality and needs to be accepted. Remember the traffic jam, the nightmare gridlock. You have to get through to the open road. You have to stay focused on getting out of a oppressive situation. Wishing that you were not stuck will certainly not be effective, just frustrating.

Rule Two: Do Not Overreact to the Situation in Front of You.
Taming perfectionism is a difficult task because more often than not, gifted kids have gifted parents who are perfectionists themselves. You, as the parent, have to stay calm. The intersection of perfectionist parent and perfectionist child complicates the problem and makes it more intense. The parent wants the child to feel comfortable about making a mistake but at the same time, the parent is very uptight about making a mistake himself of herself. Imagine that the traffic jam is not getting better and that there are helicopters ahead. All of the other drivers around you are anxious. Be careful and keep a safe distance—rushing and pushing ahead will cause an accident. Don't think the worst!!!

Rule Three: Keep Your Problem in Perspective.
The gifted child is very emotionally intense and dramatic, which makes negative feelings and behaviors seem more dire to parents. Parents have a

hard time putting the behavior of their infant, child, or teenager into perspective, which validates and encourages the negativity. Put the traffic problem into perspective. Turn on the radio or a movie for the kids and try to relax. When you model calmness, you teach your child to be calm and persistent.

Rule Four: Wait for Calm.

Eventually, your child will get tired and stop his or her negative behavior, and everyone gets a break. The traffic jam is over. And you have not made the difficulties worse by losing control. You have demonstrated the positive value of not freaking out.

When parents can't calm down, a negative behavior pattern between parent and child is established and subsequently escalates. Screaming matches between parent and child accomplish nothing. Parents need to learn how to redirect their child's anxiety and negative defensive behavior. This is imperative. Otherwise, senseless screaming matches will ensue, which does not help anyone in the family. In other words, being calm when you feel like you want to scream is often the way to start to solve a problem with your child.

WHY REDIRECTION WORKS TO DIFFUSE PERFECTIONIST TRIGGERS

Whatever a child's problem, although he or she feels it intensely and presents it dramatically, it may not be as serious as it seems to the parent who is trying too hard to be a "perfect parent." Good enough parents do better with intense children because they are psychologically minded and base their authority on insight and developmental issues rather than narcissistic expectations of what is best. For example, a toddler is upset because he wants another cookie or his toy that has fallen off the high chair. He is playing a game with dad. Unfortunately, perfect dad is looking for a teachable moment to let the child know that cookies are bad for you if you eat too many or that dad is not a slave who picks up after the child. The parent is better off offering the child a piece of fruit or taking him out of the high chair and letting him explore the room. This solution seems too obvious or too easy to the perfect parent, who is determined to impart wisdom to the upset child.

I am going to share a true story that demonstrates how redirection can calm a situation down. I work with a family with two highly gifted children who are very intense and also sometimes shy and stubborn. When the family was on vacation, both children were tired of traveling and eating in restaurants. The eight-year-old was so frustrated that she refused to go to the restaurant where the family was planning to meet friends. Elena was about to have a temper tantrum. Joshua, her older brother, started teasing her, saying she was spoiled. Just when the entire family was on the brink of a full-out meltdown, a huge black St. Bernard walked past and then sat down. Both children went to play with the dog. The potential embarrassment for the parents was over. The situation was temporarily resolved because of redirection.

Later in the week, Elena, Joshua, their mother, and I talked frankly about the situation. Elena was the first to say that the dog distracted her, which was why she did not have to have a temper tantrum. After she thought about the situation, she admitted that she should have been happy to go out for lunch. Her brother said the dog was a good distraction, and he felt ashamed of himself for teasing his sister. Joshua admitted that he was taking out some of his bad mood from earlier in the morning by teasing Elena. Mom was shocked but relieved that her children could be so clear-minded about the potential disaster, and we all felt better! The family vowed not to have too-high expectations when traveling.

Redirection is practical, realistic, and child friendly. Parents who are overly thoughtful about child rearing can entirely miss my point about redirection. In my experience, parents can be overly concerned that they are not using potential teachable moments to depart wisdom (which no one is ever interested in at the time of crisis). Or they are concerned that their child has attention deficit disorder, which is often not true at all. It is always better to discuss important issues when everyone is at least almost calm.

Another trick to avoid meltdowns is establishing what will happen next. Get some feedback about how your children feel about the activity that is about to begin. This is not a foolproof strategy, but it does establish reasonable expectations for both parents and children.

Here are some interventions that can be implemented at key points to avoid perfectionism and eventually eliminate procrastination:

1. Is my child concentrating on being stubborn and not listening?
2. Repeat the question and find out.
3. Is my child just emotionally intense, or is he being impulsive?
4. Empathize with your child and then set some realistic limits.
5. Is my child bored and frustrated, or does he or she need more stimulation?
6. Talk about what is causing his or her upset.
7. Is my child shy, or is he or she socially awkward and immature?
8. Help your child develop social skills by arranging appropriate social activities that he or she can participate in.

PERSISTENCE PREDICTS SUCCESS

Having a high IQ—being gifted—does not necessarily lead to success in the "real world." Persistence is necessary if the gifted person is going to be successful. Learning how to make mistakes and recover—that is, resilience—is crucial. Parents who can model persistence for their children will help them succeed. Often, parents are too involved in what they are doing right or wrong and miss the point of teaching their son or daughter how to just forge ahead. Persistence is different from redirection because it involves deep frustration about not getting one's own way. Parents often think that if they redirect their child or teenager, they are making progress at teaching them to keep trying. While parents avoid outbursts by redirecting, avoiding conflict with your child is important only to a certain extent. Parents can model persistent behavior for their children and talk about how they deal with frustration. Parents can point out coping skills that they use when they want to give up. Giving up and not being persistent is just giving up. Learning to learn from mistakes is very important, and parents need to learn how to teach this lesson.

GENERAL STRATEGIES TO TAME PERFECTIONISTS

1. Do not use perfectionist criteria when motivating a gifted child because doing so will intensify overachievement or underachievement and distract from the child's potential.
2. Be careful to set realistic goals and standards for the gifted child.
3. Don't transmit your own perfectionist goals and standards to the gifted child. In other words, don't overidentify with your child.
4. Understand the difference between challenging and pushing a child.
5. Learn to fruitfully advocate for your child. Avoid being your child's business manager.

CONCLUSIONS

Gifted children have unique learning problems. However, a wide variety of problems reflect a child's personality and the family structure. Identifying the problem in as much detail as possible and then working on solving it is reasonable and possible. Parents manage their child's problems. You can effectively manage by being calm, focusing on the problem, and offering appropriate rewards or child-centered consequences. Finding experts or specialists who can help you is critical. Developing a positive relationship with your child's teacher and/or tutor will make your job easier.

You can do it!

6

Parents and Schools Working Together toward Educating Gifted Children to Their Truest Potential

Choosing an elementary school for Marjorie has been one of the most challenging decisions we have had to make as parents so far.

—*Rosa*

There is no way of finding the right school by just looking at them. Choose a starting point and go from there. If it does not work out, try another school.

—*Jesse*

We bought a house in the best school district with the highest test scores. We are sure we made the best decision.

—*Marlene*

THE MOST FRUSTRATING TASK OF PARENTING: THE CHOICE OF SCHOOLS

The gifted child is our hope for our own future as a strong, balanced, and powerful nation. Scientific inventions, art, music, literature, drama, psychology, medicine, leadership, technology, and space travel (to name a few) depend on deep and creative thinkers. Unfortunately, how to develop the gifted mind is seriously ignored by our educational institutions. Perhaps some of our indifference as a society is related to the lack of a definition of giftedness. Uncertainty about what giftedness looks like is based on the varieties of giftedness that can be developed. How to meet the variety of different needs of gifted and talented children is a problem for educators.[1] To make this situation more dire, educators can have strong negative reactions to parents who claim that their child is hard to teach because he or she is gifted.[2,3] I see educational obliviousness as an ongoing nightmare that takes a great deal of courage and patience to live through. Empowering parents to successfully educate their precocious children is a crucial goal of this book.

Over and over again, I hear from moms and dads who consult with me the same old conversations about whether school officials think giftedness exists. The parent innocently says to the teacher or principal, "I think my child is having problems at school because of his giftedness." The teacher, with an apprehensive look on her face, responds in a cold and negative tone that reflects her point of view that parents say their child is gifted to explain their child's negative behavior in a positive light. "How do you know? Where is the proof? Has the child completed standardized tests?" Or the teacher might be rude and say in a mean-spirited tone, "I really cannot see what you are talking about. Your child is having a hard time completing his work." Or the teacher might say, "Your child is a problem in the classroom. He never pays attention!" Instantly, the already stressed parent is put in the corner for bringing up a concern. The teacher becomes an adversary instead of an ally. Even worse, the teacher feels stressed because gifted parents have been and continue to be stereotyped as pushy, demanding, and unreasonable. In actuality, parents do not sufficiently advocate for their gifted children. Clearly, a lack of realistic procedures through which parents can work with the schools is hard for children and parents alike.

Finding some common ground between parents, teachers, and administrators can be a very difficult task. Who in the school environment is supposed to meet the unique needs of the gifted child? According to policy, public schools are required to meet the individual learning needs of each and every child. Private schools can also use public resources to assess individual learning problems. The procedure to qualify for individual help is based on a deficiency of two years in achievement or social emotional growth. If there is not enough of a gap between the child's skills and the grade-level standards, the child does not qualify for help. Once qualification has been determined, an Individualized Educational Plan (IEP) is written by the school's team of experts, including administrators and teachers, who make recommendations for remediating the learning problem.

Schools often feel that gifted children do not have sufficient problems to warrant school involvement. Put nicely, in over 30 years of working with schools and gifted children, I have found that it is not easy to get schools to provide viable and valuable services. Both public and private schools need to be coerced into responding to the needs of the gifted. Parents have to insist that their child be evaluated and then face the scorn and disbelief of educators. Actually, parents can and should ask for a Student Success

Team meeting, which is sometimes useful. A Student Success meeting is held at private and public schools when a behavior, academic, or social emotional problem is not being resolved by parent, teacher, and student adjustments. Experts such as resource teachers, psychologists, and administrators attend this meeting to look for solutions. This meeting does not produce a formal written report that goes in the student's record. Eventually, with the help of advocates such as psychologists and consultants, a teacher at your child's school will see what you are concerned about. Hopefully, the teacher will try to listen to recommendations that will enable him or her to work more successfully with your gifted child.

Concerned and committed parents also figure out how to deal with their child's school by talking to other parents who have the same problems, reading books and doing Internet research to find strategies to follow, or working with specialists who have experience with gifted families. Visiting the schools that may work for you and your child is imperative. Promotional materials sent to parents don't tell the whole story. Friends' advice, although helpful, is not the same as meeting the people who will be working with your child.

Always be prepared for negativity when you dare to mention you have a gifted child. Actually, I believe that the double talk and confusion about standards children need to meet to be considered for a gifted program is just a diversionary tactic to wipe out the problem of the gifted child entirely. From an administrative and classroom point of view, the gifted child requires too much attention. Mainstream black and white standardized objectives and goals take precedence in private and public schools. Your child's gifted education is your problem, and you will need to find a good school that will see and respect your concerns and goals. Finding respect for your talented child can be a Herculean task.

A parent who worked tirelessly to find school placement for her gifted child shares her thoughts and actions.

While preschool was stressful, we always knew that we liked the Montessori approach for our daughter, and she thrived in an environment where she could control the pace and the concentration of her learning.

But elementary school was different. We had to choose between a very good public school and a private school; each had advantages and disadvantages. We gave the public school a chance because there were opportunities for Marjorie to make friends in the neighborhood, and we heard that the school was very good.

While Marjorie's teacher noticed from very early on that she was advanced, she told us from the beginning of the school year that she would be limited in the curriculum she could teach based on the Common Core standards that were in place. In language arts, she could differentiate to a degree, while staying within the standards, but in math, she would not be able to help Marjorie very much. The principal and teacher agreed to enrich Marjorie's experience by putting her in with first graders for a few hours every day and giving her access to the computer lab. By all standards, it seemed like these efforts should have helped, but in the end, it was not enough to keep Marjorie engaged. This seems to have affected Marjorie's social behavior, her attitude toward school, and her general feeling of disconnectedness from her peers.

We chose to move her to the private school because of its ability to differentiate, and we hope that once she is more engaged, she will be happier to be in school, which will ultimately help her socially as well.

LOOKING AT EDUCATIONAL OPTIONS

Finding the right school match for your gifted child is a long-range, ongoing issue that changes focus as your child grows into adolescence. There are so many conflicting points of view about what you should do and how to get it done. There are challenges and roadblocks all along the way. Helping your very bright child get the right educational start is truly one of the most essential and priceless gifts you can give your child. Today's parents are under increasing pressure because they are in competition with countless other parents who also want the best for their children, whether or not they are gifted. More and more parents strive to get their children on the right track very early in life by carefully selecting which toddler Mommy and Me classes to attend with their child. More parents than ever check out all the preschools in their neighborhood, attempting to give their child an enriched early childhood education. In the extreme, some parents enroll their children in "quality" preschools before they are born! These parents wrongly believe that the right preschool will ensure entrance to a good private school and down the road, this school will lead to acceptance at a prestigious college. Please understand that problems related to educating a gifted child are far more complicated than choosing the right preschool. Extra activities, family time, and play dates are as crucial, and they also provide child-centered limits. Keeping on track with your child's education is an ongoing issue. Some years are easy, and some years are very challenging.

Selecting a kindergarten presents all parents with even more options and opportunities for confusion. And getting into certain kindergartens is not as easy as getting into preschool. Sometimes, the process of getting a child into the "best" kindergarten can be more competitive than getting that same child into college. Later, decisions about middle school and high school confront both students and parents, who subsequently then concern themselves with college admittance. You may wonder if there is a connection between where children get their early education and their future educational opportunities. Of course, there is some correlation, but there are no guarantees that the "best" school will produce a self-motivated productive student. Rather, parenting that takes into account asynchronous development is crucial if a child is to develop a vision for what he or she wants to become and the skills necessary to achieve his or her goals. Optimizing your child's potential is a long road to travel with many challenges along the way.

WHAT PRIORITIES ARE MOST CRUCIAL?

Clearly, your educational choices are critical and complicated. Making a decision can be confusing. There is a general lack of agreement about what gifted children need in a school setting. What is most important? Acceleration at all costs? Prestige? Whole child development?

Acceleration

While I see acceleration as important, it can become a problem if challenges are the entire focus of your child's education. Single-minded acceleration can create emotional pressure and intensify perfectionist tendencies. Still, parents and educational researchers see challenge as crucial. Acceleration to address certain areas of talent and achievement is critical.[4]

Here is what Linda, who has a school house gifted child (an intellectually intense child who soars in classroom situations because of his or her interest in learning to read and achieve; see the chapter on intensity), has to say about acceleration, which supports my point that circumstances do not remain the same throughout your child's educational journey. *School options for the gifted are sadly nonexistent, as is witnessed by the fact that grade acceleration has become a taboo for a great many gifted students. How absurd that a resource as rich as these engaged and imaginative minds is being squandered in an attempt to keep America's classrooms "equitable."* Later in her son's life, she found a middle school that was highly accelerated. Her son blossomed with friends and academics that were very challenging. Her daughter received extra lessons after school that were accelerated, and she was equally engaged in learning.

Prestige

Prestige is a value that parents assign to schools, both private and public, for their gifted children. It is hard to argue against the point that a child educated at a top-notch school has advantages. Prestigious schools have many great teachers, highly evolved curricular and instructional interactions, and extracurricular bells and whistles. Unfortunately, more often than not, prestigious school do not focus on the needs of the perfectionist and quirky learning styles of the gifted. The match between prestigious school and child depends on how socially outgoing the child can be. Often, gifted kids are introverted and not as interested as their classmates are in mainstream ideas. Andrea, whose child was accepted at a top-of-the-line school, gradually won the argument with her husband about how stifling and anxiety-provoking the prestigious school was for their son Stephen. Andrea says:

My husband was very concerned about taking Stephen out of the presti-
gious school. It was so well thought of with so many extras that no other school
in our community could offer. It has the best reputation in the city where we
live. It was hard to believe that our son did not fit in. But the reality was that
he was way too sensitive for the bullying children and the culture of money
and pretense that was part of the school community. It was all wrong for
him. The teacher didn't get him at all. She was continually critical and pres-
sured him relentlessly. It seemed like she took the sides of the bullies because
they were from the wealthiest families.

Another parent opted for a highly gifted school. Anna wanted to send her son to the top gifted school, even though her son's preschool suggested a more progressive environment to deal with Sammy's energy and curiosity. Sammy was accepted and given the official label of highly gifted child. Unfortunately the school environment was way too strict and traditional for Sammy. Eventually, he was asked to see a psychologist for help with his behavioral enactments. Behavioral enactments include not listening to teachers and not doing schoolwork. Finally, Sammy was asked to leave. He was much happier and productive at a more progressive school because a progressive school has less rigid rules that need to be followed. Individuality is more of a value in the curriculum.

Whole Child Focus

The whole child focus is my preference because I know that gifted kids have issues with social skills. When they are able to work through these issues, they are more successful than children who are pure over-achievers or die-hard brainiacs.[5] I realize that there are drawbacks to a more progressive education. George, who has had his son in a progressive private school since kindergarten, was encouraged by how the school dealt with challenging his son. He shares:

I'm happy with the school we chose because our son is unfolding into his
own self. The school respects each child's individuality no matter how fast
or slow they are working. For example, the teacher saw, without being told,
that our son Liam was getting bored. She paired him into a higher group,
which gives him more challenging material. The school and our family form
a good partnership. We agree not to push him but to challenge him when he
is curious.

Unfortunately, by the time Liam got to middle school, George was feeling discouraged that the private progressive whole child school was not helping Liam want to achieve his potential. Fortunately, Liam's family accepted the academic school-imposed limitations and added all sorts of extra tutoring and travel in the hopes of keeping their son engaged in his giftedness and talent. Meanwhile, Liam made deep friendships, which is crucial, because he is basically a very introverted teenager.

Private, Public, Religious, and Home Schooling

Still more questions: A private school? A public school? A religious school? Home schooling? The answers to these questions vary. Indeed, the differences within the gifted category are as great or greater than variations between gifted and nongifted. In other words, because the range of variability among gifted children is so enormous, there is no way to prescribe a gifted education that will work for all children.

Some educational researchers suggest that a public education is most valuable because it exposes a gifted youngster to children of different ethnicities and cultures. Public education is available to all children. By definition, public schools are not supposed to be elitist. Yet, hidden forms of discrimination exist in public education. An emotionally intense and imaginatively intense gifted child will have difficulty with an ordinary gifted classroom, which will be too structured and focused on achievement.[6] And most likely, his or her needs for in-depth curriculum will not be met.

Within the public school system, there are different types of gifted components, ranging from weekly pullout classes to separate schools for the gifted. These vary from school district to school district and within districts, from school to school. Also, standards for admission to these gifted programs are based on achievement tests and school performance. Unfortunately, public gifted education has been very neglected in recent years because of the No Child Left Behind Act and the Common Core curriculum. An absence of an accelerated curriculum and instructional material is definitely a serious drawback for many gifted children and their concerned parents. However, some charter schools and highly gifted magnet schools can meet the needs of gifted learners. Parents need to search long and hard for these public gifted schools that take into account the whole child.

Private schools suffer from elitism because they are open only to children who can meet the entrance criteria. These privately funded schools believe in and can logically support the value of their enriched curriculum for gifted children. Private schools do have more say over what is taught and how it is taught. They tend to have a more innovative curricular approach, which can be individualized for the students who attend the school.

Private schools that are exclusively for highly gifted children believe that they provide the most challenging education. At highly gifted private schools, children are segregated with other very bright children and never need to bother with ordinary learners or lessons. In their formative years, these children are isolated from mainstream children. Often, children in these hothouses of intellectual stimulation and expectations burn out from too much pressure. I know of many teenagers who, because of too much pressure to achieve, drop out or consider suicide. Educational burn out is most often associated with high-pressure private and public gifted schools.

Religious schools are a different type of private school that often have a very traditional approach to instruction. Although religious schools can be closed minded in their approach to innovative curriculum, they often encourage skipping grades to deal with children who are very advanced. Accelerating gifted children has been shown to have positive effects on intellectual development without the feared negative social and emotional consequences. Home schooling is a new trend in educating gifted children. Some people believe that home schooling is a last resort when a child cannot be placed in a highly gifted program or accelerated to the next grade. Some experts truly believe in home schooling for profoundly gifted children with IQs above 170.[7] Home schoolers generally seek early college entrance for gifted children. Home schooling is more prevalent in rural areas.

In conclusion, the debate about the right way to educate a gifted child is longstanding.[8] There is no perfect curriculum that is right for every gifted child. You must choose carefully among your options, keeping in mind what you value in education for your child and what you can afford. Also think about these comments from parents.

My husband and I are both products of public school systems who went on to college and postgraduate schools. We never questioned that our kids would go into the public school system, though it has been a struggle at times to fight the fear that private school students are getting more and better opportunities.

Six years and two children into our local public school, I strongly believe that our gifted kids are better off for being part of the public school system. The diversity of the public school student body—racial, cultural, and economic—mirrors our community. While two local private schools offer only one classroom per grade level, there are four classrooms per grade plus a special education classroom at our local public school. The numbers alone allow for my kids to explore different social situations, find peers, and move among groups of children. The diversity allows them to learn about and adapt to their community and the world.

While gifted and talented educational (GATE) testing doesn't take place until the second semester of the second grade, both my children were recognized as gifted by their kindergarten, first grade, and second grade teachers. They were given extra work and held to higher standards. My daughter was already young for her grade, and skipping her was not an option my husband and I were willing to take. The school was supportive of our decision and found a way for her to participate in both her home classroom as well as in the grade above.

Our teachers are credentialed and tested more rigorously than private school teachers, and they undergo monthly training in curriculum changes and advancements. The teachers at our school take great care in choosing which teacher will be best for each student as they advance from grade to grade. Personality and academic interests are taken into consideration, which allows the child to grow and excel.

In addition to the GATE curriculum, our teachers seek out-of-school opportunities for the gifted kids such as county and state competitions in math, history, and art. In fourth grade and fifth grade, each classroom has two teachers: one for science and math, and one for English and social studies. The kids learn to adjust to different teaching styles and expectations, and how to share resources and collaborate with their classmates.

Our school is lucky to have tremendous parent involvement, and fundraising and grants allow us to have a violin program for all third graders, orchestra for fourth and fifth graders, and performing and visual arts programs for kindergarten through fifth graders. Field trips are an important part of the curriculum and have exposed my children to performances at Disney Hall and Pasadena Playhouse, art at the Huntington and Norton Simon museums, and hands-on experiences at jet propulsion laboratory (JPL) and Cabrillo State Beach.

My gifted children have flourished at our local public school.

SCHOOL PLACEMENT DEPENDS ON THE INDIVIDUAL FAMILY SITUATION

Each family situation really is unique. And in turn, what schools offer their students varies. Some schools are very strict, while others value creativity. I could go on and on about the different types of learning environments you can choose from within the parameters of school choice. In other words, there are some very progressive schools that are strict and some very traditional schools that are creative. But you as a parent cannot match your child with a school that will develop his or her true potential until your values about how to parent and your expectations for your child are clear. Saying this, I know that it will take you some time to decide the bottom line of what you value in an educational experience.

TEN TOP ISSUES THAT PARENTS TALK WITH ME ABOUT REGARDING SCHOOL CHOICE

1. How can I find the best school match for my child?
    Most parents are concerned about finding the best school match for their children. I help parents decide their best options by first working to understand what type of early childhood education they have chosen for their child. This information gives me insight into their values and expectations for schooling. For example, parents who choose Montessori schools are most interested in an individualized approach to education. Religious preschools stress religious values even if they are individualized. Academic preschools are very teacher directed. And, of course, there are other philosophies of early childhood. With this knowledge and an understanding of the parents' own educational experiences, I map out some choices to consider, and I review the child's developmental history.

2. How can I know if what the school says about itself is true? Are the promotional materials and tours really reflective of what goes on when the children are at school?
    I ask parents to find out what the schools they are visiting mean by individualization, social skills development, academics, diversity, community participation, and acceleration. I also suggest talking to parents who have children at the school.

3. How does a learning challenge affect school placement?
    Gifted children can have serious learning challenges ranging from autism spectrum disorder to attention deficit hyperactivity disorder (ADHD). It is best and appropriate to tell the school you are interested in about your child's issues and what help you are getting to assist the child. Some public and private schools allow children to come to school with a "shadow" to assist them in the classroom. Having the school you select want your child is very important to everyone in the family.

4. What are the dangers of labeling a child?
    One danger of labeling a child with a mental or learning disorder is that the label may prevent people from seeing that the child no longer matches the label. Labels can become self-fulfilling prophecies. A child given an overarching medical diagnosis will be more likely to have problems than a child who is seen in a positive light. As much as possible, try to describe your child's struggles in behavioral terms without labeling him or her.

5. Should the school directly reflect our cultural and religious values?
    Parents of gifted children ask this question if they themselves are religious and very aligned with their cultural identity. The answer to this question will be based on your child's level of giftedness and the school's experience working with gifted children. So there is no one answer to this question.

6. What are alternative ways of assessing giftedness?

   Alternative measures of intelligence are available to assess learners' strengths. Howard Gardner has proposed at least eight intelligences—linguistic, logical-mathematical, musical, bodily kinesthetic, spatial, inter- and intrapersonality, existential, and naturalistic.[9] Daniel Goleman has written on the importance of emotional intelligence, a critical aspect of social intelligence.[10] Robert Sternberg has developed assessment devices to measure what he thinks intelligence is, that is, analyzing, solving problems, and thinking critically.[11]

7. Is a traditional education more important than a progressive education?

   These two very different philosophies of education can cause conflict and confusion for parents. Traditionalists think that schooling should expose students to ideas that have perennial value and have withstood the test of time. The development of moral character is also a major consideration, as is the development of concern for others. The latest curricular fads and technology are seen as not essential to real learning. In contrast, progressive philosophy is oriented to the present and future, is based on multiculturalism, and encourages teamwork. It involves communities of learners, dialogue, shared experiences, and opportunities for self-discovery. A child-centered curriculum is subjective and based on projects, in contrast to traditional education, which focuses on carrying out prescriptive lessons that regulate time and sequence, limiting the breadth of what is to be experienced by the student.[12]

8. Why is individualized academic education important for gifted children?

   To understand the importance of individualized academic education, parents and educators have to look at what is meant by an academic program. Traditionally, academic programs emphasized specific achievement in prescribed content, usually as separate school subjects such as math, English, science, or history. Curriculum content was presented as teacher-directed instruction. The student attained knowledge and achievement through studying and participating in the teacher's presentations. The teacher was in charge of the students' progress through testing and classroom questions. This very rigid and directed approach is ineffective when it comes to working with the intense curiosity of a gifted child.

   In contrast, an individualized program can be academic but will emphasize the students' deep understanding of key concepts in academic fields and the ability to use these concepts in many situations. An individualized academic curriculum can be project centered. Students engage in real-world problems or unsolved problems in a given special field. Teachers are facilitators, helping students formulate the questions or problems to be addressed. Students plan their investigation and collect data, and they engage in data analysis and interpretation, presenting their findings and recommendations to other students and/or parents. Working collaboratively by sharing ideas and solutions in small and large groups is seen as the most effective way for students to learn.

9. Why and when should we consider home schooling?

   Parents who call with this question often describe their child as highly curious and talkative. They love learning and seem to soak up knowledge. Most often, they are early readers and able to do second grade work in kindergarten. Parents fear that their child will be bored in regular public schools, which have policies against acceleration. Public schools are unable to provide any gifted education until third grade. Private schools are often not open-minded about gifted children. The highly gifted schools are sometimes too pressured and structured. Home schooling parents feel as if they were forced out of public and private schools very early. They make a practical decision to pursue home schooling.

   Gifted home schooling is very different than religious home schooling. Mothers who have gifted children create online networks to share useful tools and teaching strategies. Indeed, there are virtual communities for parents of gifted children. Also, homeschoolers can attend various enrichment activities and have regular play dates with other gifted children at local parks and museums. These exceptional children do well in highly individualized learning programs.

10. What is the difference between a gifted child with asynchronous development and a child who is called twice exceptional?

    Most likely, this distinction should be made by a psychologist, learning specialist, or developmental pediatrician. Twice exceptional children have disabilities that need specific interventions that may not be possible in a regularly paced classroom, although there is a trend toward mainstreaming all children, which helps the twice exceptional child stay in a regular classroom. Special classes and schools, both public and private, thrive as they seek to meet twice exceptional special needs issues.

    Home schooling is one valuable tool that is used with twice exceptional children.

    The benefit of home schooling is that parents are able to select a curriculum to meet their children's particular strengths and weaknesses. Choosing the right method for your child, from a very structured school at home approach to a more relaxed structure, is possible. Parents have the freedom to combine multiple methods and curricula. A wealth of information about available options can be found online and through teaching and learning stores.

In conclusion, there are serious issues and concerns most parents have to face when choosing a school. Understanding and acknowledging your own family values and expectations is the first step in making an informed decision about the right match for your child. In other words, you have to be deliberate and honest about your educational values and what expectations you have for your child's school. The second step is finding out as much as you can about educational options and opportunities. Every school is unique. The school you select will have a set curriculum and standards for your child. Remember, you are the consumer. And as the consumer, you should be aware of what you are getting yourself into. Be prepared to complain and to accept compromises.

QUESTIONS TO ASK AT INTERVIEWS

Interviews are always stressful for parents because of the evaluative position of the administrators. However, you will gain power and knowledge if you have your own questions that show that you have thought about what you want in your child's learning environment. Well-considered questions reflect your interest and capacity for engagement in your child's school. Good questions lead to a positive presentation of your family life and your parenting skills. Here are some questions you may want to ask.

1. How are children grouped in the classroom?

    The answer to this question is critical because it shows the school's real commitment to individualized and differentiated curriculum and instruction. If you sense that all children are expected to sit at their desks and work at the same pace and learn the same material, you will know that individualization is just a promotional marketing tool. If, on the other hand, there is a lot of emphasis on small group learning and project-centered assignments, you will know that the school actually takes individualization of learning seriously. Gifted kids need individualization at school.

2. How does the school deal with competition between children and families when it arises?

    This question will help you understand how seriously the administration believes in the importance of individual development. If competition is encouraged for any reason, you might look elsewhere. Gifted children are perfectionists, and competition can lead the children to procrastinate or give up if they cannot be the best. Schools that value families' cultural differences are more likely to be able to deal with parent-parent and child-child competition.

3. How do you accelerate children in their areas of talent?

    This is a way of asking indirectly if they have experience working with gifted children. Look for an answer that acknowledges the importance of acceleration. Asynchronous development—learning highs and lows—is related to acceleration. The school you choose should be able to address gifted children's uneven learning styles.

4. How do you deal with children who are shy, quiet, or introverted?

    Gifted kids, in general, tend to be shy or to have difficulty with their peer group. The answer to this question will help you understand how the school deals with socialization issues. You want to find a school that is very concerned about social development. If there is an emphasis on sports and competition as a critical form of social interactions, the school is not right for your child. Most gifted children are not that comfortable with sports unless they are gifted in sports. Try to find a school that values performance, art, and cultural diversity.

5. What is the role of parents in the school community?

    In both public and private schools, parents' influence is variable and essential. There are extremes. Sometimes, because of budget cuts, parents can become too involved in the classroom. Parental overinvolvement can erode the power of teachers and administrators. Parents can create a hotbed for gossip about what is right or wrong with each child, as if the parents were experts. On the other hand, when parents are left out of the classroom entirely, some enriching and meaningful connections are lost. When parents are relegated to the back burner, what is special about your child and family may be ignored. Parental involvement is crucial.

6. How are community events handled?

All schools have fundraisers. Get a sense of how the school handles fundraising. See if you can understand if you will feel comfortable as a contributor in the community of parents. Remember that contributing your time is as important as your financial assistance. Participating in community events is very important for your child and the family, as it creates a crucial sense of meaning and acceptance.

7. What policies are followed when bullying occurs at school?

If admission personnel say that there is no bullying at their school, they are not being honest; they are trying to present a false front to entice parents. I have never seen a school that does not experience some form of bullying. The school you are looking at should be open and honest enough to explain how teachers and administrators handle these kinds of negative social experiences. Resolving bullying problems is a learning experience for your child that he or she will most likely have to deal with in his or her educational journey.

8. How are parent-teacher conferences handled?

This is a tricky question, and answers range from rigid standards to very open-ended standards. Try to get a sense of whether teachers listen to you and make changes that you suggest or if they just mirror what you are saying, pretending they are taking you seriously and then just proceeding as if the conference had not taken place. Often, other parents at the school will know which teachers are open minded and which are not interested in parents' concerns.

9. How do you deal with the special problems of gifted children when outside experts are involved?

Learning how teachers and administrators work with experts is crucial. You need to have open lines of communication with the administrators, teachers, and specialists who work with your child. You need to get some type of answer to this question that reflects past experiences with gifted kids.

WHEN YOUR CHOICES DON'T WORK OUT THE WAY YOU'D HOPED

Believe me, there is always a problem, no matter how thoughtful and careful you are about school choice. You never get everything you want. The school is more costly than you can afford. The drive is too far. Admission committees won't accept children with diagnostic labels. Compromise is always part of the end result and your choice.

Problems arise when anxious parents expect too much from the school. While the school is aware of the "overinvolved parent" and has its own strategies to put parents in their place, parents need to assess the problem realistically by looking at the bad and good points of what is going on in the classroom. If you are totally stressed out about classroom learning, hiring an outside consultant can really help you decide how to deal with the problems you and your child are experiencing. Boredom, a cold and indifferent teacher, and social awkwardness are the most common problems you should not over-react to immediately. It also helps to be cautious and optimistic. Children pick up your concerns and react by not trying hard enough. So, do not go overboard about whatever is not going the way you planned.

Common disappointments with school choice usually involve the following:

1. Anxious parents who are expecting way too much to begin with Parents whose child did not get into the school of their choice because of the child's special learning needs
2. Parents whose child did not get into the school of their choice because of the child's special learning needs
3. Parents who were conflicted over their choice and did not follow a well-organized plan of action
4. Parents who did not spend enough time investigating school options
5. A child unable to handle the pace of the school and subsequent adjustment issues
6. Separation anxiety or plain anxiety in the student

Common unexpectedly good outcomes include:

1. Your child does well at the new school because of extra resources that you did not expect would be so helpful.
2. The school and the teacher are unusually sensitive to the needs of gifted children.
3. Kids and parents are extremely friendly, and your child makes lots of friends.
4. You and your spouse are happy with the results and see each other's point of view

WHAT GIFTED PARENTS NEED TO KNOW ABOUT THEIR CHILD'S STRENGTHS AND CHALLENGES TO FOSTER COLLABORATION BETWEEN TEACHER AND PARENTS

I have said this over and over again: Giftedness comes in all varieties. Like a garden in bloom with no two flowers exactly the same, the garden of talent is expressed in very different ways. Even identical twins, who are assumed to have nearly identical genes, demonstrate different aspects of giftedness.[13] Therefore, you must wonder why standardized tests of intelligence such as the Wechsler Scales (WISC) are used to identify giftedness. Here is the answer. The subtest scores of the WISC look at different aspects of intellectual development and paint a unique picture of the child being assessed. Behavioral checklists, qualitative analysis, and parent questionnaires all provide useful information about how your child is gifted and where your child's challenges lurk. Books are written about what types of school different levels and types of giftedness require. You should research levels of giftedness and make your own decision.[14]

After your initial introduction to the school, not the first words out of your mouth, work to enlighten the school staff about what is special about your son or daughter. When you learn how your child will most likely function at the school from psychological assessments and qualitative analysis, explain your sense of your child as a learner to the teachers and specialists who work with you. Even explain the giftedness that has been assessed in your child to your child in words that your child can understand. Yes, it is a relief for children to know that they have "gifts." Keep in mind that understanding your child's way of learning is an ongoing process. In other words, you cannot understand the extent of your child's giftedness in one hour with a psychologist or even in one year with a teacher. Giftedness is a profound quality that requires ongoing understanding and attention.

Marilyn, a mother who questioned the value of an assessment for her kindergartener, was delighted to have gone beyond her reservations about getting her son evaluated for giftedness. She shares:

Now that I know what the problem is and that it is related to Henry's type of emotional intensity, I can talk with the teacher and be transparent, instead of being afraid that my child is just not gifted. Getting the assessment was a turning point with our connection with the school and understanding Henry's issues.

Get as much specific detail as you can from experts in assessment. Gifted children have asynchronous development, that is, they have uneven patterns of development. They very often need challenge for their talents and other types of intervention for their areas of weakness. When your child is evaluated for giftedness, be sure to ask the evaluator about your child's specific intellectual potential, personality development, self-concept, learning styles, achievement, and interests. Having this detailed information will help you communicate with the teacher about your child's educational options. Listen to what the teacher has to say; he or she will have invaluable insights as well.

Dealing with the school will be an ongoing challenge. Some years will be calm and focused on learning, and other years will be more difficult because of problems with peers, teacher-child misunderstandings, or specific academic challenges. Since these challenges will continue throughout your child's education experience, we'll explore them in more detail in the next section.

LEARN HOW TO DEAL WITH YOUR CHILD'S SCHOOL

You will always face issues with your child's school. You need to take off your rose-colored glasses and decide how you can best handle them. The top issues I hear about from parents who consult with me are boredom, separation anxiety, perfectionism, social awkwardness, bossy behavior, bullying, and daydreaming. The top complaints that I hear about from teachers are related to parents who are working and leave the nanny and aftercare specialists to do the real work of parenting, or the parents who are too involved and always demanding that their child be the center of attention. In between are some solvable parent-teacher problems.

Work with the Teacher and Show Respect

Probably the most important factor in the school environment is your child's teacher, the human element and the nurturer of your child's intellectual and emotional growth along with social development. Never underestimate the teacher's pivotal role. It is quite important that the teacher and your child develop rapport, that is, some intellectual and emotional connection.

Often, teachers and students don't get along. This can lead to serious conflicts between the parents, the child, and the teacher. This is a very difficult problem to solve. Miraca Gross, a well-known teacher of gifted children, writes:

> As a teacher and academic working in gifted education, I have become sadly familiar with the cutting down to size of children who develop at a faster pace or attain higher levels of achievement than their agepeers. Perhaps these children offend our egalitarian principles and our sense of what is fit. Perhaps they threaten us as teachers; few of us encounter, with perfect equanimity, a young child whose capacity to learn is considerably greater than our own. Perhaps they are what we would wish to be, and are not. Perhaps they merely irritate us; gardening would be so much easier if all children progressed at the same rate. For whatever reason, intellectually gifted children are, more often than not, held back in their learning to conform to the pace of other children in their class. In Australia the practice is so explicitly recognized that it even has a special name: "cutting down the tall poppies."[15]

Truly, the perceptions of your child's teacher are crucial. When my son Richard, who was an early reader, was in kindergarten, he was tested for the gifted program because his teacher Mrs. Hanf thought that he was gifted. Richard was placed in the pullout gifted program. More important than this placement was the reality that every morning he could hardly wait to get to school and work with Mrs. Hanf. At the end of kindergarten, Richard was placed with Mrs. Olsen, who had the reputation of being a boring teacher. Mrs. Olsen put Richard in remedial reading, where Richard read on his own his chapter books from home. Mrs. Olsen called to tell me that Richard was not paying attention. She thought my son had ADHD. I knew Richard was just bored. Immediately, I sensed that I was facing a big problem and that the neighborhood school that went with our new house was not going to work out. Fortunately, I was able to put him into a private school that individualized curriculum and was interested in each and every child. This was the best decision I ever made. And I was lucky because now, getting into private schools is a long and tricky process.

Here is what Linette, a parent in my group, writes about this very issue: *Highly gifted children pose a real challenge to teachers, and not all teachers are prepared to meet that challenge. It is very easy to misdiagnose the learning difficulties that often accompany a high degree of giftedness—boredom can be mistaken for attention deficit, or the desire for efficient shortcuts can be perceived as cognitive difficulty. Gifted children are also often sensitive and pessimistic, and a teacher's attempts to correct and instruct may be misperceived by the gifted child as hostile and unreasonable. The result is sometimes a disastrous downward spiral when the teacher tries to "fix" the gifted child by demanding conformance and focus beyond the child's ability, leaving the child to react by withdrawing or challenging the teacher, causing the teacher to try still harder to fix the child and elicit "normal" performance. Unhappiness results all around.*

Madeline, a parent in my support group, shares her thoughts on why the teacher is important: *The teacher controls the environment that either encourages or discourages your child's interest in learning. However obvious this may seem, the results of teacher actions can have a great impact, even relative to actions that seem quite minor. For example, the seating arrangement chosen by the teacher can work actively to support or diminish interest in learning. Seating a bright introverted child next to a loud hyperactive child may cause the quiet child to feel intimidated and anxious, or it may destroy the introverted child's ability to appropriately engage in classroom activities. Of course, this seating arrangement may help the teacher because the introvert probably doesn't engage in the negative behavior, therefore limiting its contagious tendency. The arrangement may even help the loud child focus a little better, but the teacher's decision to use the introverted child in this way can have a strong negative effect for that bright child for the life of the offending seating arrangement, a school year, or possibly much longer. Additionally, the teacher may influence your child's self-esteem through verbal and nonverbal feedback, and the health of a child's self-esteem is known to significantly affect family, educational, and social life.*

John adds: *If too many of the teachers decision's are in favor of ease, "having all the kids on the same page," focusing on academically challenged children, standardized test scores, and the teacher's physical or mental test—emotional opinion—then the outcome of the school year could be significantly reduced. On the other hand, teachers focused on helping your child happily achieve to the level of his potential, with the stamina and knowledge of how to make this happen, can make a lasting impression that can significantly benefit the child for years to come.*

Sandra shares: *The teacher is important because your child will spend an average of 20 to 30 hours a week with this person. They had better be the correct teacher for your gifted child. The teacher must be smart—smart enough to catch onto the "slippery" behavior of very intelligent children. They will try and can pull anything over on anybody and everyone. The teacher must have tremendous acuity. Also consider that children who are highly gifted and have special needs are highly sensitive and vulnerable. They might need special attention, and it might not be easy to figure out what will help them.*

The parents of the highly gifted are generally the same as their children but all grown up with none of the coping skills and considerations we are trying to give our gifted children. We as parents can be very unreasonable. The teacher must bridge us all.

Lauren adds: *My daughter is very sensitive to personalities, so who the teacher is matters. It affects her comfort level, which in turn affects how hard she works in class. This includes a range from tackling harder work to "dumbing" herself down. The teacher needs to be keenly aware of each child's abilities and help them all live up to their capabilities.*

Susan, a mother who wrote to me online about her confusion about what she can do to get challenge into her child's school day says: *I know how much pressure/stress public teachers are under, especially in Texas. However, on the other hand, I do feel that maybe Mrs. E is not keenly aware of gifted children and their special needs. Thus, no special attention, extra advanced materials, or care is given. Or maybe it's just that she does not have the energy or time to give to a gifted child in her class. She's got a handful already with 24 kids plus some disruptive girls to try to quiet down. My friend did tell me her son's teacher (years ago) gave her son advanced materials in class and took care of his needs. But can we ask Mrs. E to do that, or what can I ask her to do? I certainly don't want to start a stir, nor do I want to be annoying parent who appears to be wanting something special for her kid.*

Make Personal Connections within the School Community

Get involved so that you know what is going on without appearing to be overinvolved and a know it all. Parents should have a pivotal role in elementary school as a support for the school they select for their child. Parents have to be involved in something personal that gives their child and family a sense of uniqueness and identity. School is an important social structure for your child and the rest of your family. It will be your new extended family and community. By becoming involved at your child's school, you will meet other parents, teachers, and administrators who will help you and your child make a successful transition to the new school and its community. You will learn from the members of your new community valuable parenting lessons and strategies that will make you a more effective parent. Play dates will come out of being involved with other parents. Support for all kinds of issues related to day-to-day parenting will be available.

PREPARE YOURSELF FOR THE ISSUES OF HOMEWORK

Here is how gifted children show how smart they really are. They get out of their homework. I have never encountered a gifted child who didn't dislike homework. Parents, teachers, sisters, and brothers are all privy to the problems precocious kids have with their homework. Be clear about your expectations for your child's homework activities. Make homework a priority as soon as possible so that your child will be prepared to take on the responsibility of completing school work. Check your child's homework at a regular time every day. Realize that smart children have a hard time with homework that is boring. You will need to work through problems of boredom and the need for highly stimulating work. Parents are responsible for figuring out how to get the child to do homework. And yes, even if they know better, gifted children will directly or indirectly try to get out of their assignments.

To eliminate some homework issues, find a school that does not focus exclusively on grades. When an opportunity comes up, talk with the teacher about how sensitive gifted children can be and how negative comments about homework affect your child. Try to explain the meaning of school and homework to your child. You might say to your child, "Work is mom and dad's homework." Play games with your child about his or her homework when it is difficult. Make a list of next steps to try in solving a particular problem. Hopefully, taking this proactive approach will circumvent your child's perfectionist tendencies and the ensuing anxiety, avoidance, and procrastination that can develop.

THINK ABOUT YOUR CHILD'S PEER GROUP

To repeat myself again, gifted children have unique socialization issues. Basically, it is very important to make sure your child has friends to play with several afternoons a week and on weekends. If your child is having problems establishing friendships, try to understand why. Talk to your child's teachers to get their insights and suggestions on who at school might be a good playmate.

Do not let your child become isolated. Find enrichment classes that reflect your child's interests and then help him or her make friends within this group. Involve your child in athletics that are group centered, even though gifted children can be reluctant to play sports. Remember, the latest research suggests that gifted children are likely to make friends who are older than they are. While older friends are normal, you need to be aware that your child is just a child and keep track of what is going on when they play with friends.

Extended family, such as cousins who are the same age, provides social experiences that are enormously useful for developing your child's sense of self. Participating in religious and community groups teaches children about their religious, ethnic, and cultural identity, which in turn helps develop pride and a sense of belonging outside of the family. Camp experiences are also critical because your child will learn to be a part of a group away from home. Social maturity derives from different types of peer interactions. The greater the variety of social experiences children have, the better off they will be as they climb the school ladder and meet different children from different home environments.

Parents who attend my parenting groups have shared their experiences with peer group issues.

Rosa says, *Marjorie often complains about the games that the kids play on the playground, saying that they are "baby" or "silly" games. There are moments when she tries to orchestrate the group so that they are playing the games that she would like to play, manipulating who and when people can play. The teacher said that Marjorie has the ability to see three steps ahead of any child and tries to use her insight to get what she wants.*

When she talks about the kids, there isn't any one child or group that she really wants to be with, and she can get dissatisfied that she doesn't fit in with any of the groups on the playground. She says the boys won't play with her, and the girls are often playing games she gets bored with; this leaves her feeling like she doesn't fit in.

George says, *Miles is very shy and has a hard time making friends. The teachers at our school have helped him develop friendships. Still, I am very concerned that he doesn't have many long-term friendships. I always take my son camping with a family we have known for many years. Having this extra outside friend for Miles has helped him to be more out going.*

Susan says, *Nathan is very sensitive to rejection and also wants every activity to go his way. This combination makes for lots of confusion at our house abut play dates. Nathan wants friends to come over and play, but he also wants to only play the games he wants to play. We keep talking to Nathan about what it means to be a friend and how he has to compromise. We keep having play dates, but it is very very frustrating because we can never predict the outcome of a play date. Jack goes with his dad to Boy Scouts, and he has lots of friends there. But Jack has no friends at school. He reads a book at recess or goes to the library. He daydreams during class*

*time. We have talked with the teacher and principal, which has not helped
at all. We are considering changing schools so that he can have friends to
play with and enjoy the school day more.*

THE NEED FOR ACCELERATION AND ENRICHMENT

The latest research suggests that acceleration is an educational
intervention that allows gifted children who are working at a faster pace
to move as quickly as they need to through a traditional curriculum.
Acceleration can be an individualized or a large or small group approach.
Acceleration does not mean pushing a child. It does not mean forcing a
child to learn advanced material or to interact with older children before
he or she is ready. Indeed, it is the exact opposite. Acceleration is about
appropriate educational planning. It is about matching the level of complexity of the curriculum with the child's readiness and motivation. When
acceleration is being considered for a child, online education is often seen
as an effective option.

Acceleration is sometimes criticized because it separates students from
their peer group. There is a lack of empirical research to support the notion
that separation from age or grade-level peers leads to adjustment or achievement problems. The issue of acceleration is very complicated, and acceleration should be individualized for each child. The brighter the gifted child, the
more he or she will need to be advanced to the highest challenge level. While
schools with gifted components can offer acceleration, parents need to find
private classes that provide their child intellectual and creative stimulation
in their specific areas of interest.

After-school acceleration and enrichment are critical if you want to
develop your child's true potential. Find mentors who have experience with
gifted children and classes that your child is interested in and wants to
attend. Make commitments to extra family activities that are challenging
and fun. Take an exploratory point of view as you search for what matches
your child's interests most authentically. While grandparents, friends, and
neighbors will make suggestions, remember to check your child's interest
in the extra activity. You will know from your child's reactions if he or she
enjoys the extras you are providing.

Family travel can be an excellent way to expose your children to great
adventures and new cultures, life styles, and ideas that they would not
encounter at home. Visiting with relatives and friends who have different
values is also useful in teaching your child about the world outside of home.
Inspiration comes from traveling and visiting museums and natural wonders. Ask your children what they want to explore and try to implement their
suggestions as often as possible when you travel.

CONCLUSIONS

Finding the right school for your gifted child is a challenging task that requires you to consider different variables—making a realistic plan, checking out your options, filling out the application, seeing the school, and making a choice. And eventually, you will find yourself making compromises. Consider what you value in education. Ask yourself some important questions:

1. What kind of educational experience do I want for my child?
2. Am I interested in a more innovative curriculum that is child centered and project centered, or a traditionally focused school? Why?
3. Should the school I choose look at my child's developmental readiness? Why?
4. Do I believe all children learn at the same rate?
5. Do I want the same type of educational experience for my child as I had? Why?
6. Do I want an educational experience for my child that is the opposite of what I experienced? Why?
7. What is best for our family? Public school or private school?

   Look at the advantages of public school, which include:

   Diversity of students

   Special services for all children with special needs

   More access for parents in the classroom

   Free tuition

   Structured gifted programs

   Peer interaction with children in the neighborhood

   Look at the advantages of private schools, which include:

   Smaller classes

   A more enriched, refined, focused, and developed curriculum

   Special enrichment classes in the arts, science, language, theater, sports, music, computer technology, and travel experiences

Take into account practical matters such as:

1. How much can you afford?
2. How much time will it take to get your child to school?
3. Will your spouse be able to help with the driving arrangements?
4. Will your child attend the neighborhood school and walk?

INTERACTIVE TOOLS TO HELP YOU

Think about and use the following interactive tools to help you understand and draw conclusions about your unique family needs and what kind of school you want for your child.

My Priorities in Choice of School

The school's:	Rate from 1 (less important) to 5 (most important)
1. Prestige in the community	_____
2. Convenience for parents' work schedule	_____
3. Learning technologies and classroom methodologies	_____
4. Community involvement with cultural differences	_____
5. Networking between parents and children	_____
6. Reinforcement of family safety and values	_____
7. Multicultural experiences	_____
8. Progressive education	_____
9. Response to special needs	_____
10. Emphasis on math and reading	_____
11. Emphasis on sports over art	_____
12. Gifted programs	_____
13. Acceleration plans in areas of strength	_____
14. Emphasis on exercise and outdoor activities	_____
15. Ecological awareness programs	_____

Preliminary Evaluation of a School under Consideration
(Make site observation with interviews of contact parent and student attending the school)
Which Best Characterizes This School?

New Views of Learning	Old Views of Learning
Language	
Taught through social conversation	Taught by modeling proper academic speech
Young child's speech is elaborated upon, e.g., Child: "big dog" Teacher: "Yes, the big dog is jumping."	Teacher affirms or corrects the child's response
Content	
Focus is on *how* to learn, how to ask questions and act in variety of settings	Focus is on *what* to learn, facts and information
Personalized Learning	
Children add to lessons with their own stories related to the topics at hand	Children adhere to answering questions and completing assignments given in texts and workbooks without personal elaboration
Ability	
Individual differences are attributed to children's prior experiences	Teacher believes individuals differ because of innate ability
Errors in Performance	
Errors are seen as learning opportunities	Errors are marked wrong and feedback is given to the child on how to correct them
Errors reflect child's perception, which teachers try to understand	
Learning task is messy, requiring child to "figure out" how to achieve good performance	Learning task is broken down by teacher into simple steps for the parts that make up the task
Participation	
Multiple opportunities: group discussions, whole class lessons, paired activities, games, and social activities	Children learn to attend to the teacher, follow instructions, and engage in guided practice and application of newly taught concepts

(*continued*)

(Continued)

New Views of Learning	Old Views of Learning
Collaboration	
Children help each other, each one contributing to the common goal	Each child does own work; children compare their levels of performance
Authority	
Children judge their own work, prepare alternative solutions, and seek evidence for facts presented	Teacher judges and scores child's work Standard rubrics are used in assigning grades
Assessment	
Children have many ways to show what they know: drawing, acting, writing, building, etc.	Both standardized tests and teacher-made tests show what the child has learned
Parent-Teacher Conference	
Teacher listens to parents' concerns	Teacher controls the conference, apprehensive about parents who know too much about education and schooling
Teacher acts upon home-centered information as way to support both parent and child	
Child participates in the conference	Child is exempted from parent-teacher conference

7

Everyday Issues of Gifted Kids and Their Families

Books about how to parent don't generally apply to gifted children and their parents. Curiosity, intellect, intensity, and overexcitabilities can make gifted kids' reactivity to situational stressors more profound. In reality, precocious kids' reactions can be very hard to understand. Bullying, achievement pressure, family stress, parental insecurities, worry, anxiety, depression, use of electronics, and sibling rivalry take on a different dimension of "craziness" for your gifted child. This chapter examines how gifted kids tend to deal with contemporary issues that families face in our frantic and chaotic world.

BULLYING

Gifted children are more susceptible to bullying because of their emotional intensity and sensitivity to how other children react to them. Preferring to relate to older children or adults who have similar interests, gifted children come across as quirky to their same-age peers. Because of their unique social development, their friends might see them as victims, nerds, bossy, or withdrawn bookworms. To counter or put into perspective the tendency of peers to see their intense friends as weird, intellectual interests motivate gifted kids to think about what is going on with their friends. For example, Julia a precocious five-year-old, told me, "They think I am weird because I want to dissect a frog, and they just want to play with their dolls. It's ok with me; I am more scientific than they are." Fortunately for parents and teachers, smart children have the ability and the desire to talk in detail about what is bothering them. Getting a social problem such as bullying out in the open is the first step.

Backing up just a bit, I define bullying as the conscious abuse of power over someone who is not able to fight back because of emotional, mental, or physical limitations. Bullying is a form of harassment. In this hostile relationship, there is an aggressor and a victim. Bullying is common in schools all over the world. Research-based interventions to prevent bullying and stop it when it starts are readily available to schools and the educators in charge. Controlling bullying is possible if schools and parents work together.[1]

Bullying is most often based on differences in culture, ethnicity, and socioeconomic status in the school community. Parental expectations, insecurities, and conflicts about social injustices are transmitted to children directly and indirectly. Unknowingly, and sometimes directly, parents assign the role of victim or aggressor to their child based on the social identity they held growing up. Social competitiveness is always present when bullying is occurring. There is no way to really eradicate this game of one-upmanship. Understanding how you feel about bullying, harassment, and discrimination is a step toward reversing this moral problem that is rooted so deeply in our culture. Taking a stand against bullying will make a difference because it will show your gifted child that you care about how other people are treated.[2]

Proactively protecting gifted kids from bullying is possible. Schools that value individual development are more likely to deal effectively with bullies because competition between students is neither highlighted nor valued. Children who feel loved and competent are less likely to want to be aggressive or victimized. Saying that good enough parenting helps reduce bullying is not enough. There is always a parent or child who needs to be top dog, which begins the cycle in earnest. Bullying can start on the first day of school. Thus, I suggest that parents keep a careful eye out for social injustices, even if careful consideration was given to school choice.

Private and public schools' promotional materials can be both honest and deceptive. In their promotional materials, all schools promote goodwill between children, faculty, and parents. Still, bullying is commonplace, and promotional materials can be both honest and deceptive. It is hard to predict what will get the cycle of bullying started. In my experience, parents who value high achievement are jealous of other parents who have gifted children. Always, there are personal and interpersonal relationships with classmates, teachers, administrators and other children's parents that will not come into "the life of the school yard" until school starts. In other words, what causes children or their parents to feel competitive and mean spirited is hard to predict. But escalating unkind behavior is common in all types of school communities. Religious schools, public and private schools, and very elitist schools are not only susceptible to but do have issues of bullying and discrimination to deal with and hopefully resolve as they come up.[3]

Parents sometimes have a hard time believing that visiting their school of choice, reading its mission statement, attending school welcome events, and even talking to other parents who already sent their children to the school is not enough to predict their child's happiness and social development success. Well, I can tell you from my experience with families and schools for over 30 years that promotional materials and first introductions are never enough. What one set of parents values for their child may be very different from what another family values or expects. Differences in attitude, expectations, and values in addition to administrative policies determine the course of the school year, including your child's intellectual and emotional growth, and bullying. When one family wants to have the smartest child, there will be problems. I will illustrate other predictable bullying precursors in the following text.

The Need for Prestige among Gifted Parents Contributes to Bullying

Recently, I was invited to a promotional event to meet the new staff at a school that I talk with families about considering for their gifted children. I heard the following outrageous and shocking story between parents in line for coffee. Jean told Ellen the following and waited eagerly for her reaction. Helen's son Stuart got accepted into the primary grades last year at a particularly prestigious school. Helen said that she noticed as the school year progressed that Stuart seemed to have fewer and fewer toys in his bedroom. Helen figured out, from talking to the other mothers, that Stuart was giving his toys away so that the boys in his kindergarten class who were being bullies would leave him alone. Stuart was buying his way out of being teased. This kindhearted five-year-old was learning that giving away his special possessions was a way to fit in and make friends. Stuart was being bullied even though his prestigious school had promised it did not tolerate bullying.

I was shocked that Helen was not up in arms with the teachers and administrators about the seriousness of this bullying. I said to her, "You must be enraged to be paying $30,000 a year for this type of educational community." But Helen wanted to be part of the prestigious school's high-status "family." She turned a blind eye to the bullying issue.

By overvaluing the reputation of the school, this mother was undermining her son's sense of himself. Gaining social acceptance through identifying with status-conscious educators and parents was way too important to this family. This search for status can seriously affect gifted children, creating longstanding depression and deep feelings of emptiness. Teenagers who cut themselves for attention to feel alive exemplify how this type of depression can emerge in adolescence. Children pressured by parents to do well in highly prestigious schools too often burn out and/or drop out in college.[4]

Children who get involved in mean girl debacles are usually very insecure because they lack love and/or nurturing; that is, they have attachment issues with mom, dad, or both parents. Perhaps mom is too busy at work to pay attention to her child, or dad is indifferent. At school, children act out insecurity in power struggles between girls over who is prettiest, strongest, smartest, richest, most popular, talented, and so on. These children believe that by showing themselves to be the most powerful and important, they will feel better about themselves. Insecure girls bully other children to gain power, self-esteem, and good feelings they do not get at home. In turn, victims feel that their inadequacies are just being validated by the peer group, and they take this social abuse. It is hard to stop this dynamic when it starts because victim and aggressor are getting some emotional feedback that is absent in their homes and that confirms their sense of themselves.[5]

Mean girl stories are rampant, even in elementary schools. Problems between girls are usually related to social acceptance and the child's self esteem. Gifted girls can be quirky, so they have a harder time fitting in. Sometimes, gifted girls try too hard to fit in with other girls, and they are perceived as obnoxious and given the cold shoulder. Sometimes, gifted girls dumb them self down just to fit in. And sometimes, they just give up and read in the library or the corner of the classroom.[6] I always encourage parents to encourage their daughters to get out onto the playground, even though I love books and reading. The following story illustrates a typical playground disaster that involved mean girl bullying when teachers were out of sight.

I worked with a gifted child, Dannella, who because of a loving but unconventional and chaotic home environment was teased in kindergarten and first grade. The secular and religious school administrators felt that Dannella was being teased because she was immature. And Danny did bring her stuffed rabbit to school. She was often seen sucking her thumb. Rabbis, teachers, and administrators recommended that Dannella repeat first grade. Marsha and Stan, Dannella's parents, knew how bright their child was, so they decided to put their daughter into a different kind of school. They hoped that the new school would stop the problem of Dannella being teased by bossy girls. In truth, Dannella was afraid of the new students and liked to go to the library for recess. Eventually, Danny's reluctance to socialize on the playground was addressed. However, Danny was still being bullied.

I came to understand after countless conversations with teachers, administrators, Dannella's parents, and Dannella herself that the family environment was not structured enough to give Danny a good sense of herself. Her uncertainty about herself made her vulnerable to bullying. The second school she attended was proactive about bullying, with direct interventions in the classroom and on the playground. All of the parents and children in the classroom met with consultants to learn new strategies to relate to one another. The mean girl bullying problem was contained; it really took a village to resolve this underhanded and complicated problem.

By telling this story, I am suggesting that it really is easier to provide your child with a solid emotional foundation based on your love and support than to reverse bullying. Gifted children are very sensitive to criticism because of their perfectionist tendencies, so the more loved and understood they feel, the less vulnerable they will be.[7]

Gifted Boys and Sports

Gifted boys are often bullied because they do not like to compete in sports. Be aware of this issue and stress the importance of physical activities. Help your son participate and learn how to participate in team sports. If stronger athletes start to tease, talk with your child and the coach about the importance of valuing the entire team. If your child is reluctant to play sports, try to find a school at which the culture of sports does not dominate other social activities.

Racial and Socioeconomic Bullying

The child who is the odd man out in terms of race or socioeconomic status is too often bullied. For example, I worked with a gifted third grader whose family was considerably wealthier than the other families at his school. Beginning in kindergarten, this child was picked on for being the rich kid. Parents and administrators worked tirelessly to solve this bullying problem. When I met with this seven-year-old child, he knew more about how to deal with bullies than I did. However, even with a strong knowledge base, his reaction was to take on the punk identity of the other children at school. And he decided to dumb himself down and got into the bad habit of not doing his work at school and home. Over the years, Roger fell farther and farther behind.

Roger shared with me his thoughts on bullying. He said, *Listen, it was tough when I was bullied. None of the books or strategies they teach you are going to work no matter what they tell you. Adults have forgotten what it is to be a kid. Talking about your feelings with kids from different kinds of families will not help. You see, these classmates come from broken homes. Touch them at their level, not your level. They are going to try to break you and make you cry like their fathers do to them. They want to humiliate you and make you afraid. Do not go to the principal; she will only make it worse. Stare them in the eye and show them that you want to be left alone.*

At my new school, I feel respected. There is zero tolerance for bullying. When an issue arises, the teacher talks to all the children together. Bullying is not a kid issue. It is a family issue. Parents and teachers have to solve the issue. At my old school, I think I came from a background that was very different from the other children. I was picked on. Here, we are working out problems in the classroom, and I feel safer and more important.

There are more stories that I could tell about the bullying that goes on at every school I have ever consulted with over the years; suffice it to say, bullying is a problem at all public and private schools because it is part of how children, who learn from their parents' examples, are socialized.[8] How the issue is dealt with is in the hands of teachers, administrators, and specialists. Keep this in mind as you think about how your child is doing at school. Having friends is certainly an issue for gifted children, who naturally prefer adults who understand them better than their same-aged peers. If your child is unhappy about something that is going on at school, you can safely suspect that bullying might be part of the problem. If bullying is happening, talk about it with the school and your child. Don't let others' mean behavior erode your child's love of learning and school. Confront the bullying issue with tact and persistence. Look into your heart and mind to see how you are contributing to or diffusing social injustice issues.

Here are some ways the parents I work with advise that you may be able to detect bullying:

1. Your child has bad dreams or considerable anxiety about going to school.
2. Your child tells you, "No one plays with me."
3. Your child is reluctant to do homework or other school-related projects.
4. Your child is hyperactive or withdrawn at school.
5. Your child is very anxious at home and has problems sleeping.
6. The teacher tells you that your child is not making friends.

What Parents Can Do

In general, socialization is the key to helping your son or daughter avoid bullying. Encourage your child to develop friendship in your neighborhood, at school, and in the community. Extended family friendships are also extremely important in the development of social skills and social confidence.

Specifically, parents should show interest and concern about what is distressing their son or daughter. Ignoring the problem will not help it go away. Rather, parental avoidance will escalate the humiliation your child is experiencing and make him or her feel more alone and fearful. Here are some specific steps you can take to address bullying:

1. Talk to your child calmly about the details—who, where, and when—of the bullying that is going on at school.
2. If applicable, share your own experiences of being bullied when you were a child; doing so normalizes your child's pain and to enables him or her to connect with and trust you.
3. If you remain concerned that your child is being treated unfairly, ask to meet with the teacher.

4. Working with the teacher and your child, develop strategies to redirect mean-spirited, negative behavior.
5. Make play dates with children at your child's at school, in the neighborhood, or at extracurricular activities to build your child's social self-confidence.
6. If the bullying persists, ask for a meeting with the principal to find out more about school policy on handling bullying. All schools have outside resources for dealing with bullies. Make sure the specialists are being used in your child's classroom.
7. If you are not satisfied with intervention results, seek out the advice and help of a psychologist or an educational consultant who, if necessary, can help you find a new school for your child.
8. It is very important for your child to work with a trained mental health professional as he or she addresses the emotional effects of bullying so that your child's self-confidence is rebuilt and strategies to avoid bullying are understood and developed.

UNDERACHIEVEMENT IN GIFTED CHILDREN AND TEENAGERS

Gifted individuals are often stereotyped as being weird high achievers, underachievers, or dropouts from the education establishment. All of these stereotypes are just superficial judgments that are inaccurate and untrue. In reality, some very bright individuals choose to not live in the limelight and pursue careers that give them happiness, peace, and fulfillment[9]—consider gifted people who pursue charitable work. Certainly, gifted individuals can be underachievers for so many different reasons; however, systematically understanding the nature of underachievement seems to be almost impossible.[10] Keeping the illusive definition and nature of underachievement in mind, here are common variables that I have seen in my more than 30 years of professional observation that contribute to underachievement:

1. Low self-concept and lack of positive motivation toward learning and school
2. Family negativity toward the child that undermines or does not promote self-confidence in areas of talent, academics, or achievement
3. Parenting styles that oppose and contradict one another so that the child does not have to complete his or her schoolwork
4. School match that is not effective for the child's specific learning needs
5. Peer group influences that are negative toward school achievement
6. Home life that is too stressed and chaotic to allow the child to concentrate on school
7. Gifted children are not necessarily interested in being high achieving students
8. Cultural values that do not endorse achievement

Schooling—the right school match—always contributes to the quality of achievement, which I have addressed throughout this book. The level of giftedness often determines how mismatched the school and child will be, which predicts achievement. For example, a profoundly gifted child (with an IQ of 160 or above) in a typical classroom environment will give up from boredom and thus underachieve.[11] Strategies to combat gifted under-achievement tendencies from a curricular point of view exist and can be implemented if family or public school funding is available.[12] At this time, gifted education is not a priority in considerations of public school policy, thus increasing underachievement tendencies.

The most important point in this discussion is that underachievement can be reversed through a detailed analysis of emotional issues and learning problems. In other words, knowing the problems that your child is having with learning and then targeting strategies to correct them is critical. The teacher-student match is so essential because of the gifted child's sensi-tivity. Finding a gifted teacher, gifted tutor, or gifted therapist to work with your child is important. Gifted professionals can identify with your child's quirks and figure out how to help your child overcome fears because they have been through your child's struggles.[13]

Overcoming by working through parenting challenges, which is the sub-ject of this book, will contribute to maximizing the potential of our gifted children, thereby reducing underachievement. A theme related to under-achievement is the unidentified gifted child who is lost in the school system because his or her parents are too busy or unaware of the child's talents and special gifts to be advocates. Children with parents who suspect they are gifted usually get more help with their challenges than children with parents who are oblivious to their unique learning styles and talents. Identifying gifted children without the benefit of parental insights is a critical topic for educators working with underprivileged children. Early assessment via observing behavioral char-acteristics (which I described in Chapter 1), without psychological testing, seems to be the most effective approach classroom teachers can take. Still, teacher-directed acknowledgement of giftedness can have limited results because assessing giftedness is very complicated. Teachers should not be given the role of psychologist or developmental pediatrician. Misdiagnosing gifted-ness as autism spectrum disorder or attention deficit disorder is very common if the evaluator does not have enough knowledge about giftedness. Treating a gifted person with the wrong strategies will make problems with achievement and relating to others even more confusing.

While underachievement may be caused by asynchronous development, underdeveloped potential is a very different issue. Underachievement involves deep motivational problems such as learned helplessness, lack of self-esteem, inadequate parenting, and parental and cultural values that do not endorse achievement. Poverty that creates day-to-day stress related to just getting by its very nature dismisses those who advocate for talent. Asynchronous development is a more basic and unfettered part of the self. When the common learning problems of gifted children are attended to, underachievement is less likely to occur, no matter the family's socioeco-nomic status (see Chapter 4).

From my own clinical and consulting experiences working with children and their families, I can attest that underachievement is a red flag that something is wrong at home or at school. Your child is feeling inadequate, misunderstood, or fearful and is acting out this unhappiness with himself or herself—or with others—by giving up on school work. In other words, there is an emotional component to underachievement. What I recommend to the families who come to see me about underachievement is that they try to figure out what is wrong at home and at school. These are questions that I am concerned with:

1. What are their child-centered consequences for unacceptable behavior?
2. Do parents spend enough quality time with their child?
3. Is the school a good match?
4. Is outside special help necessary?
5. Would an IEP be useful?

Parents often have long, complicated answers when I ask what is wrong. The feeling of being drowned by problems is both common and harmful. I prioritize the presenting academic problems. I start by understanding the worst part of the problem. This sounds straightforward, but sometimes, parents and kids are overwhelmed and need help focusing on moving ahead. Seeing progress is critical. What does not help is making the problem bigger than it really is. Try to stay calm and be positive that your child will overcome his or her achievement issues. Your job becomes understanding what works and what does not work. In general, pressure and criticism backfire. Baby steps that are clear and manageable will get you on the right track and keep you focused on your journey.

ELECTRONIC USAGE: VIDEO GAMES AND THE INTERNET

Unsupervised and unlimited video games and use of the Internet are very dangerous for gifted children, who can easily get addicted to the feedback and entertainment available to them from electronic devices. Getting children to do homework and participate in family time can become an ongoing struggle for moms and dads who set up family rules and structure. Of course, electronic addiction has different levels. And, as parents I work with point out, video games can help children learn to socialize. However, I must caution you that too much screen time is dangerous. In worst-case scenarios, children and teenagers prefer to stay home and play video games and don't go to school.[14]

Because they are so precocious, figuring out how to access material that is too mature for them is not a problem. Rather, gifted kids are challenged by figuring out how to get around the rules. In most instances, children and teenagers are a lot more advanced than their parents want to believe.

They can easily become overstimulated by adult ideas and stories, or they can figure out how to use their parents' credit cards and charge large amounts without permission. The hazards of electronics are endless for clever and curious children who, if motivated, will figure out most anything they want to on their electronic devises.

The other problem with electronic overuse is that it limits time spent studying and socializing with friends and family. Helping out in the kitchen or the garden, or entertaining other children in the family, is ignored. Getting involved with outdoor activities, community service, clubs, and creativity goes by the wayside. Reading, listening to music, and practicing instruments plays second fiddle to cyberspace. Parents will someday regret that they used television and movies as babysitters. Interpersonal relationships develop your child's personality in a way that passive attention to movies and videos cannot, even if they are interactive. Grandparents, aunts, uncles, and babysitters not only watch your children but they show kids what it means to be responsible and to listen to others. They can also provide comfort and advice that parents are not in the position to offer.

FAMILY STRESS

Life histories of gifted individuals illustrate the importance of a balanced home life, confidence in one's child, and a serious commitment to a parenting vision.[15] Further, balance in family life is crucial if vital relationships are to be established and nurtured. For balance to evolve, there must be respect for each individual in the family. Just as you learn to listen to each of your children in a special way, your children need to learn to listen to you and to respect you and appreciate your efforts. Teaching children the importance of communication requires a lot of effort, thoughtfulness, understanding, and patience. Snap judgments and quick actions undermine communication and balance in the family. Rigid and dogmatic thinking halts the balance and cooperative spirit derived from communication. Labeling a child genius, sensitive child, or learning disabled not only undermines their individuality but creates expectations and forced inequality in family life. Harmless as labels may seem at first glance, this type of imposed identity can be very destructive to the child and to the family.

Gifted children are more intellectual, insightful, and sensitive. For these reasons, they may feel like their lives are out of control more intensely than their same-age peers. The birth of a new baby, a family illness, a job loss, a move, a divorce—each is an external event that naturally affects any child's sense of security and well-being. When an unordinary stress arises, parents are, to some extent, naturally distracted and less available to provide emotional support and practical day-to-day care of their children. Gifted children are especially sensitive to changes and transitions, and they can react strongly and negatively to stressful family events. The best way to approach highly charged issues is with concern and appropriate information. It is important to remember that your child may be smart and compassionate, but he or she is not your friend or your support system. Work on taking care of your child's concerns. Do not have your smart child listen to your own issues, even if he or she offers to and can understand. Find a therapist or a good friend to help you process your own suffering. Remaining the parent in stressful situations is necessary if problems are to be solved in a healthy and functional way.

WORRY AND ANTICIPATORY ANXIETY

Sensitivity to big ideas and what can go wrong is inevitable and normal for gifted kids. Worry can get the best of bright children, who see the big picture more easily than less insightful children.

Smart children can imagine a lot of negative possibilities. Often, they suffer from anticipatory anxiety in new situations such as school, enrichment activities, vacation, camp, or even a trip to an amusement park. You will have to learn to accept and deal with their anticipatory anxiety.[16] Here are some strategies that will calm everyone down:

1. Prepare your child for what to expect in new situations. Talk to your child about what worries them and makes them feel anxious.
2. Give your child coping strategies that relate to their concerns and reduce anxiety.
3. Keep your answers simple and child focused; giving smart kids too much information can be confusing and can provoke anxiety.
4. Even though they seem so eager for knowledge, do not underestimate their capacity to imagine what will go wrong.
5. In turn, be prepared for their genuine happiness and pride when they master new situations.

Do not confuse your anxiety with your child's anxiety, as doing so will create more chaos and drama. Parents frequently worry about different issues then their children do. For example, Sandy is afraid of roller coasters because her heart races too quickly on the ride. The other children in her class have fun on them, which makes Sandy feel confused and inadequate. She wonders why she is different. Mom and dad are worried that Sandy will never outgrow her problem and that she will always feel like an outsider. Interestingly, neither of these parents experienced a good social life as children. They are projecting their anxiety onto their daughter. Sandy's anxiety is much more limited and contained then her parents' anxiety.

If your child does not out grow his or her anxiety, it may be helpful to seek consultations from mental health experts in the field of psychology. Ignoring or avoiding your child's issues with anxiety and worrying will certainly make their vulnerabilities seem more unmanageable and serious. Mental health professionals will help your child identify feelings and thoughts that underlie their anxiety. Together, therapist and child will make a plan to conquer these fears. As children sees progress in conquering fears, they will develop confidence in putting fearful thoughts into perspective.

SIBLING RIVALRY—A CRY FOR HELP?

It is common for gifted children to feel and speak negatively about a younger brother or sister. Sensitive and emotionally intense kids can take the birth of a brother or a sister as a serious threat to their place in the family, no matter how reassuring parents are about their unconditional love. Take this truth to heart and be realistic when your child feels unloved and left out. Ask yourself if their frustration is being misplaced on their younger sibling. Try to help them feel loved, even if and when you want to scream in frustration. Children who are very insightful do well with explanations, but in such a life-altering situation, explanations are not enough. So, after you have discussed the pros and cons of the new baby, move on to finding a certain toy, a special parent-child date, or a trip that will quell their sense of loss. Remember that emotionally, they are younger than they sound when they are talking with you about life. While they may act like big shots, they need plenty of hugs and reassurance.

Sibling rivalry is a very normal situation that often continues on and on. Brothers and sisters develop their own attachments, which are profound and nourishing even when they complain about one another and fight. It is very important to treat each child as an individual and very special in his or her own ways. Favoring the child you think is smarter is always a mistake, as it puts pressure on the favored child and takes away the other sibling's ambition. Here are some thoughts about how to contain fighting between siblings:

1. Value family balance and communication.
2. Encourage prosocial behavior.
3. Have firm but individual consequences for fighting between siblings.
4. Do not overreact emotionally to fighting.

EXISTENTIAL DEPRESSION

Introspection is a hallmark of bright children and teenagers who want to know the answers to serious questions about the world. Although less intellectual children do not ask these questions, you can be sure your gifted child will ask the following:

Why is there homelessness?
Why doesn't my friend Amy have a daddy?

Why are some children at our church so hungry and need our food?
Where is God?

When their curious, idealistic, and self-righteous minds get answers to these deep questions, your children can become disillusioned about life and depressed about its ultimate meaning.[17] These feelings are real but also transient. Give your children simple answers that calm them down. If your children are very reactive, be very careful about what you expose them to on television and in general. In young children, depression about problems with the world is not as serious as with adolescents. Teenagers can figure out how to be self-destructive or get involved with drug culture, pornography, and other illegal behaviors. Parents with teenagers who seem to be suffering from lack of energy and despondent moods should seek help from mental health professionals.

PARENT TRAPS AND PLAYGROUND POLITICS

Playground politics are based on unsolicited educational information, gossip, and advice from mothers and fathers whose children go to school with your children. Unfortunately, what some unpsychological people might call idle talk can really determine how well your child fares in school. Playground politics begin in Mommy and Me classes and continue through college applications and acceptances. I know the power of playground politicians because I have two children who are out of the box. We have lived through negative experiences related to gossip and unasked-for advise. I have consulted with parents and facilitated support groups to help parents cope with this unusual form of bullying that undermines family happiness and self-confidence. Playground politics should be contended with and hopefully irradiated, or at least put into perspective.

Parenting traps are set by well-meaning parents who can be jealous gossipmongers on the playground, in carpool lines, and on smart phones. Seriously avoid the following parenting traps if you want your son or daughter to reach their true potential.

Trap #1: Gifted children are very self-sufficient and can raise themselves. This commandment belongs in your circular file (wastebasket) under senseless information. It is given from nongifted parents of nongifted children who are jealous of your child. Disregard further input from these playground politicians who are not tuned into your challenges. Playground politicians cannot even imagine what kind of problems you have to deal with. Gifted children have so much energy, curiosity, and intensity that they need to be managed by parents who care about and understand who they are and what they need. Left to their own devices, gifted children can become lost and confused about both home and school issues. They can become highly skilled troublemakers or seriously angry and despondent.

Trap #2: You can raise a gifted child alone. This advice is as ridiculous as it sounds. It is a way for jealous parents of nongifted children to humiliate you and marginalize your struggles. Gifted children are kids with special needs. Parents need the support of spouses, friends, family, and specialists to maintain a calm and thoughtful perspective on their children's development. Group support from other parents with gifted kids is invaluable. Making decisions with your spouse or partner is a must. When a parent is isolated and feels drained, his or her child will have too much freedom to wreak havoc on home life and schoolwork. It takes a village to raise a gifted child.

Trap #3: It is okay to brag about your gifted child. No way—bragging can lead to your child having problems relating to the world. Only "accessory parents" see their gifted children as status symbols. The child's talents are something to show off like a Gucci bag or Rolls Royce. These types of parents want to be with other status-conscious parent who are competing to have the smartest child. Accessory parents want to be the center of attention and use their children to be successful in this realm.

And, of course, gossiping parents believe that bragging is okay. It is their way of elevating their self-esteem. But bragging about your child creates unspoken pressures and expectations. You need to contain your pride to small groups of people—grandparents, your therapist, and your support group. Have your small circle of friends promise they will *not* talk with acquaintances at the market or mall about your child.

Bragging can create a false sense of self that your child has to live up to. Living up to your expectations takes away from what your child wants for himself of herself. This is a serious problem that you want to avoid at all costs. Your options, when you become your child's agent, are limited to psychotherapy for narcissistic behavior, burnout, or self-destructive behavior. Let your child find his or her own way. If children want to brag about themselves, let them. And listen and be proud that they are impressed with themselves, as this is your role when it comes to bragging.

Trap #4: Your child is so gifted that school will be easy. Nothing is further from the truth. Boredom and dumbing themselves down to fit in are very common problems that schools and parents have to deal with when children are precocious. Learning to do simple everyday tasks can be very difficult for curious children, who want to be tuned into their intellect and imagination.[18] Having to learn to struggle and learn how to learn what does not come naturally are inevitable for bright enlightened minds. School can be a nightmare if special needs are not attended to correctly. Re-read Chapter 4 if you have forgotten the common learning problems of gifted kids.

Trap # 5: You should give your child everything you did not get as a child. I wrote about the dangers and consequences of overidentification between parent and child in the first three chapters of this book. So you must know that I am totally against this small-minded and self-serving parent trap that can gain power on the playground. You need to see yourself as very different from your child and in charge of final decisions. Does your child need the fanciest bike at school because you wish you had had one? The answer is certainly no. Don't confuse what you wanted for yourself with what you think your child needs. If you do, you will get trapped in an endless cycle of unhappiness with your son or daughter.

Trap # 6: There is a perfect school in your community that will meet your child's every need. Well, the preceding two chapters of this book are about how complicated it is to find the school that is good enough for your child. Hoping that you can find the perfect school is just a form of naive thinking. Well, maybe in your fantasy there is a perfect school, but not in your neighborhood or mine. Moms and dads who believe this nonsense are missing some important problems or haven't read this book. For those who believe that the gifted school at the top of hill is the best, think again. There is rejection and bullying and humiliation at this castle, and it is hard to get over when it is over. In other words, children who are *hothoused* with too many gifted children do not learn to get along with other children who are not as quick and serious as they are.

Trap # 7: You must devote your entire life to your gifted child. Parents who are too involved with their children have not lived their own dreams, or they are holding onto their children because of an unhappy childhood. The first problem with this parent trap is that your child will think you are at their beck and call, and they will text or call you all the time instead of trying to solve their own problems. Most likely, you are teaching your child to give up easily. Learned helplessness is a serious motivational problem. Children who are served by helicopter parents become adults who are power hungry and self important. Your children need you as a role model they can emulate and be proud of when they are not with you. In any case, the empty nest is real, and you will need to do more in your life than be a parent.

Trap # 8: Your gifted child can probably run the house better than you can. I have heard playground politicians joke about this very idea in a serious way. My own mother gave away her power to my older brother who, although a certifiable genius and total know it all, was not at all prepared to deal with his indomitable twin sisters. I know mother regrets that she trusted his judgment more than her own.

Today, you in no way want to give away your authority. Research highlights how bossy and know it all gifted kids can be. Judgment always lags behind reasoning. You are in charge of making big decisions. While smart kids do have good ideas and choices they can make in many areas, some decisions are just for parents.

Trap #9: You can solve every problem that comes your way. Everyone needs help, but parents of gifted kids need more help learning how to nurture their child then other parents do. Perfectly solving the problems of gifted children is impossible. No one can be perfect. No one can win every argument and always be calm. You will be dreadfully trapped in stress and disappointment if you give yourself so much power and authority.

CONCLUSIONS

Guiding your son or daughter through childhood and adolescence is a challenging endeavor. There will be high points and seemingly desperate situations. When you come to learn through trial and error what works with your child, you will find you are on the right road. Nevertheless, roadblocks will appear to confuse you and make you question your judgment. These unexpected roadblocks are important, though they are frustrating. Setbacks allow you to think about your parenting strategies and learn from your mistakes. Model positive behavior for your child when you make a mistake. Teach your son or daughter how to learn from life's normal roadblocks. The issues discussed in this chapter will come up in everyday life. Learn to manage problems even if you cannot solve them perfectly.

8

Maximizing Your Child's Potential

The biggest challenge by far is not my three gifted children themselves ... It is the society we live in that does not understand these little gems. I have found over the years that I get to engage in two types of challenges under this umbrella. Number one involves identifying who my child is all be myself because not many others have any real knowledge of gifted kids. The number two struggle has to do with fighting others about what and who my child is not ... labels that don't fit at all, but they are sure it is this or that. But they are so wrong ... gifted is just not on their list. If the focus could be on my actual child, it would eliminate half the battle. It is a challenge to not get so wrapped up in labels that don't fit.

—Jennifer

STRATEGIES FOR SOLVING GIFTED CHILDREN'S CHALLENGES

Writing down a formal procedure for being an effective parent of a spirited, challenging, gifted child is impossible because of the countless types of gifted children and families in our world. Making this disclosure up front about my reluctance to make up and give general advice, I am going to suggest some strategies that empower parents to find solutions to their particular parenting challenges.

Strategy 1: Understand Your Child's Intensity and Overexcitabilities

Remember that all gifted children are unique. Some are intellectual and can be called "schoolhouse" gifted. Others who are artistic and creative are imaginatively gifted. Giftedness is also seen in sports, music, art, drama, and leadership. Gifted children who have learning disabilities or other types of mental or social problems are twice exceptional—gifted and special needs. The more you understand the roots of your child's talents, the more able you will be to help them. Knowing a score on an IQ test is never enough information to have. Read and talk to experts to get a real understanding of your child's unique gifts.

Strategy 2: Know Your Child's Strengths and Challenges

Evaluate your child's intellectual, imaginative, creative, and emotional development with the support of a psychologist, teacher, or gifted specialist. Try to avoid professionals who do not have training with gifted children. Refer to observational tools that are available on the Internet. Alternatively, read the many books that have been written about how to assess giftedness. When you have some broad ideas of your child's strengths and problem areas, make some plans to bring out the best in your child. As important, address challenges and learn to scaffold your child's problem areas. Help from tutors and other specialists who work with gifted children is useful.

Strategy 3: Stop Wishing Your Child Were Different

Live in your parenting reality, no matter how challenging it might be. Really think about and then evaluate your reaction and your family's reaction to raising a gifted child. Is your reaction realistic? Is it too over the top? Or is it too filled with dread? Try to be realistic about your child's issues as they arise. Take advantage of close friends or a therapy to deal with your fantasy of what might go right or wrong. Develop a sense of your child as an individual who is very separate from yourself. Work out realistic expectations for parenting with your support group. Read Chapter 2 again and again.

Strategy 4: Approach Parenting with a Calm and Reasonable Attitude

Perfectionistic parenting creates anxiety for both child and parent. Learn what it really means to be a good enough parent. You might read my book *Raising Gifted Kids* for a complete explanation. Understand that overfocusing on your child in both positive and negative ways is very counterproductive. Gifted children are very sensitive to their parents' moods and expectations. If they see you anxious, worried, angry, or sad, they will react with you. When you are calm, it is much easier to parent, especially to gifted children. When something goes wrong at home or at school, look at the details that need to be attended to instead of over-reacting out of fear and anxiety. Ignoring a challenge makes it harder to handle and resolve. Please read Chapter 2 again.

Strategy 5: Knowledge Is an Important Part of Making Good Decisions

Remember that knowledge is power. Learn as much as you can about giftedness by reading books and online articles. Attend gifted conferences for parents. Learn from other parents and teachers about how to be a successful parent. Apply your newfound knowledge to your parenting style. While knowledge is not as valuable as the experience of wisdom, it is still essential.

Strategy 6: Develop a Cohesive Support Network

Search out a trustworthy support system that will listen to your problems without making decisions for you. Spouses, your parents and sisters and brothers, other parents with gifted kids, teachers, therapists, psychologists, pediatricians, and experts in gifted children can all be helpful when you need support. Your supportive others will help you stay focused on the real issues. Remember: It takes a village to raise a gifted child. It also takes a great deal of energy to find others who understand your struggles.

Strategy 7: Invest Thoughtfulness, Time, and Energy on School Choice

Carefully choose a school for your child that will meet his or her intellectual, social, and emotional needs. This is not an easy task because there are not a lot of schools that really want to deal with the issues that gifted children often experience at school. Throughout this book, I explain issues parents face as they try their best to educate their child. Chapters 5 and 6 deal directly with what you need to understand so that you can make good decisions about school choice.

Strategy 8: Social Interactions for Your Child Are Critical

Never ever underestimate the importance children's social development. Gifted kids prefer to be friends with adults or older children. They can become too engrossed in reading, computer, or other special interests. There must be a balance between passions and making friendships. You cannot overdo the friendship component of your gifted child's emotional and intellectual development.

Strategy 9: Work with Your Spouse or Parenting Partner on Shared Goals and Rules

Shared family values, goals, and rules along with a predictable family structure are essential to your child's mental health. This type of cohesiveness can be achieved only via communication between parenting partners. While it is inevitable that parents see to direct actions and behaviors through different lenses, parents have to agree on the basics. Stable home environments lead to more secure and calm gifted children.

Strategy 10: Educate Your Child's Teachers

In a stance of cooperativeness, talk to your child's teachers. Explain your child's passions and struggles in a noncombative way. The teacher-child interaction is a very strong predictor of your child's success in school. Really reach out to the teacher for advice. Help in the classroom and support the teacher's special interests and projects.

Strategy 11: Acceleration in Areas of Talent Is Extremely Important

When you have a good enough picture of your child's strengths and talents and you are working on issues as well, think about acceleration. Research indicates that children who are accelerated in their areas of interest are more successful than those who are not given these types of opportunities.[1]

CONCLUDING THOUGHTS

Always remember that your gifted child will have special learning and emotional challenges that can be conquered only when you face them head on. Being a good enough parent is far superior to being a perfect parent when you are raising a precocious and spirited child. Find a support group to help you. Do the best you can, given the circumstances of your life. And remember, your best will always differ from other parents and friends who are close to you. Remember that some years will run smoothly and some years will be rough and hard to contend with. Parenting is an ongoing responsibility that changes as you and your children grow. Try to change your perspective as your child grows.

Notes

CHAPTER 1

1. Silverman, L. K., 2013
2. Sternberg, R. J., & Davidson, J. E., 1986
3. Winner, E., 1997
4. Delisle, J., 2014
5. Roeper, A., 1995
6. Silverman, L. K., 2013
7. Webb, J. et al., 2005
8. Rimm, S. B., 1995
9. Morelock, M. J., 1992
10. Klein, B., 2007
11. Webb, J. T., & DeVries, A. R., 1998

CHAPTER 2

1. Joseph, J., 2015
2. Klein, B., 2012
3. Siegle, D., 2013
4. Ruf, D., 2005
5. Fonesca, C., 2011
6. Siegle, D., 2012
7. Winnicott, D., 1960
8. Peters, D., 2013

CHAPTER 3

1. Stern, D., 1985
2. Mahler, M. et al., 1975
3. Alexander, F., & Morton, T., 1980
4. Chess, S., & Thomas, A., 1999
5. Miller, A., 1996
6. Winnicott, D., 1970
7. Seigle, D., 2013

8. Winnicott, D., 1970
9. Socarides, D., & Stolorow, R., 1984
10. Miller, A., 1996

CHAPTER 4

1. Dabrowski, K., & Piechowski, M. M., 1977
2. Daniels, S., & Piechowski, M. M., 2008
3. Webb, J. et al., 2005
4. Baum, S. M., & Owen, S.V., 2004
5. Klein, B., 2007
6. Daniels, S., 2008
7. Silverman, I., 2013
8. Webb, J. T. A., 2013
9. Dabrowski, K., & Piechowski, M. M., 1977

CHAPTER 5

1. Klein, B., 2007
2. Silverman, L. K., 2013
3. Gross, M., 1999
4. Cain, S., 2012

CHAPTER 6

1. Delisle, J., 2014
2. Kaufman, S. B., 2012
3. Klein, B., 2007
4. Colangelo, N. et al., 2004
5. Neihart, M., 1999
6. Kaufman, S. B., 2012
7. Ruf, D., 2005
8. Silverman, L. K., 2013
9. Gardner, H., 1993
10. Goleman, D., 1995
11. Sternberg, R. J., & Davidson, J. E., 1986
12. McNeil, J., 2014
13. Klein, B., 2012
14. Ruf, D., 2005
15. Gross, M., 1999

CHAPTER 7

1. Silverman, L. K., 2013
2. Cross, T. L., 2004
3. Klein, B., 2007

4. Webb, J. T. A., 2013

5. Kaplan, S., & Cannon, M., 2010

6. Clark, B., 2012

7. Siegle, D., 2013

8. Kaplan, S., & Cannon, M., 2010

9. Silverman, L. K., 2013

10. Reis, S., & McCoach, M., 2000

11. Ruf, D., 2005

12. Kaplan, S., & Cannon, M., 2010

13. Siegle, D., 2013

14. Delisle, J., 2014

15. Goertzel, T. G., and Hansen, A., 2004

16. Peters, D., 2013

17. Webb, J. T. A., 2013

18. Delisle, J., 2014

CHAPTER 8

1. Delisle, J., 2014

Bibliography

Alexander, Frances, and Morton, Thomas. *Trends*. New York: Bison Press, 1980.

Baum, S. M., and Owen, S. V. *To Be Gifted and Learning Disabled: Strategies for Helping Bright Students with LD, ADHD and More*. Mansfield Center, CT: Creative Learning Press, 2004.

Bell, R. *Child's Effects on Adults*. Hillsdale, NJ: Halstead Press, 1977.

Bloom, B. (Ed.). *Developing Talent in Young People*. New York: Ballantine Books, 1985.

Cain, Susan. *Quiet: The Power of Introverts in a World That Can't Stop Talking*. New York, NY: Crown, 2012.

Chess, S., and Thomas, A. *Goodness of Fit: Clinical Applications from Infancy through Adult Life*. Philadelphia: Brunner/Mazel, 1999.

Clark, B. *Growing Up Gifted*. New York: Macmillan, 1991.

Clark, B. *Growing Up Gifted*. Upper Saddle River, NJ: Pearson, 2012.

Colangelo, N., Assouline, S. F., Pearson, and Gross, M. *A Nation Divided: How Schools Hold Back America's Brightest Students* (Vols. 1–2). Iowa City: Connie Belu and Jacqueline N. Black International Center for Gifted Education and Talent Development, 2004.

Colangelo, N., and Brower, P. Labeling Gifted Youngsters: Long-Term Impact on Families. *Gifted Child Quarterly, 31*, 75–78, 1987.

Colangelo, N., and Fleuridas, C. The Abdication of Childhood: Special Issue. Counseling the Gifted and Talented. *Journal of Counseling Development, 64*(9), 561–563, 1986.

Colangelo, Nicholas. Counseling Gifted Students. In *Handbook of Gifted Education*, edited by Nichols Colangelo and Gary A. Davis (pp. 120–160). Boston: Allyn and Bacon, 1991, 1997, 2003.

Colangelo, Nicholas, and David F. Dettmann. A Review of Research on Parents and Families of Gifted Children. *Exceptional Children, 50*(1), 20–27, 1983.

Cross, T. L. The Rage of Gifted Students. In *On the Social and Emotional Lives of Gifted Children: Issues and Factors in Their Psychological Development*, edited by T. Cross (2nd ed., pp. 109–114). Waco, TX: Prufrock Press, 2004.

Dabrowski, K., and Piechowski, M. M. *Theory of Levels of Emotional Development* (Vol. 1). Oceanside, NY: Dabor Science, 1977.

Daniels, S., and Piechowski, M. M. *Living with Intensity: Understanding the Sensitivity, Excitability and Emotional Development of the Gifted Child*. Scottsdale, AZ: Great Potential Press, 2008.

Davidson, J., and Davidson, B. *Genius Denied: How to Stop Wasting Our Brightest Young Minds.* New York: Simon and Schuster, 2004.

Davis, G. A., and Rimm, S. *Education of the Gifted and Talented.* Englewood Cliffs, NJ: Prentice-Hall, 1985.

Delisle, J. R. Death with Honors: Suicide among Gifted Adolescents. *Journal of Counseling and Development, 64,* 558–560, 1986.

Delisle, James. *Dumbing Down America: The War on Our Nation's Brightest Minds (and What We Can Do to Fight Back).* Waco, TX: Prufock Press, 2014.

Fonseca, Christina. *Emotional Intensity in Gifted Students: Helping Kids Cope with Explosive Feelings.* Waco, TX: Prufock Press, 2011.

Gagné, F. Toward a Differentiated Model of Giftedness and Talent. In *Handbook of Gifted Education,* edited by N. Colangelo and G. A. Davis (pp. 65–80). Boston: Allyn and Bacon, 1991.

Gagné, F. Hidden Meaning of the "Talent Development" Concept. *Educational Forum, 59*(4), 349–362, 1995.

Gardner, H. *Frames of Mind: The Theory of Multiple Intelligences.* New York: Basic Books, 1983.

Gardner, H. *Multiple Intelligences: The Theory in Practice.* New York: Basic Books, 1993.

Gardner, H., and Wolf, C. The Fruits of Asynchrony: Creativity from a Psychological Point of View. *Adolescent Psychiatry, 15,* 106–123, 1988.

Gardner, Howard. *Frames of Mind: The Theory of Multiple Intelligences,* 10th ed. New York: Basic Books, 1993.

Gardner, Howard. *Extraordinary Minds, Masterminds.* New York: Basic Books, 1997.

Goertzel, T. G., and Hansen, A. *Cradles of Eminence.* Scottsdale, AZ: Great Potential Press, 2004.

Goleman, Daniel. *Emotional Intelligence: Why It Can Matter more than IQ.* New York: Bantam Book, 1995.

Gross, Miraca. Small Poppies: Highly Gifted Children in Early Years. *Roeper Review, 21*(3), 207–214, 1999.

Halsted, J.W. *Some of My Best Friends Are Books: Guiding Gifted Readers from Pre-School through High School* (2nd ed.). Scottsdale, AZ: Great Potential Press, 2002.

Hunsaker, Scott (Ed.). *Identification: The Theory and Practice of Identifying Students for Gifted and Talented Services.* Waco, TX: Prufrock Press, 2012.

Joseph, J. *The Trouble with Twin Studies: A Reassessment of Twin Research in the Social and Behavioral Sciences.* New York: Routledge, 2015.

Kaplan, S., and Cannon, M. *Curriculum Development Kit for Gifted and Advanced Learners.* Waco, TX: Prufrock Press, 2010.

Kaufman, S. B. Who Is Currently Identified as Gifted in the United States? Psychology Today, 2012.

Kerr, B. A. *Smart Girls: A New Psychology of Girls, Women, and Giftedness.* Scottsdale, AZ: Great Potential Press, 1997.

Kerr, B. A. *Smart Boys: Giftedness, Manhood, and the Search for Meaning.* Scottsdale, AZ: Great Potential Press, 2001.

Klein, B. *Raising Gifted Kids: Everything You Need to Know to Help Your Exceptional Child Thrive.* New York: Amacom, 2007.

Klein, B. *Alone in the Mirror.* New York: Routledge, 2012.

Mahler, M., Pine, F., and Bergman, A. *The Psychological Truth of the Human Infant.* New York: Basic Books, 1975.

McNeil, J. *Contemporary Curriculum: In Thought and Action.* New York: Wiley, 2014.

Miller, A. *The Drama of the Gifted Child: The Search for the True Self* (rev. ed.). New York: Basic Books, 1996.

Morelock, M. J. Giftedness: The View from Within. *Understanding Our Gifted* 4(2), 1, 11–15, 1992.

Neihart, M. The Impact of Giftedness on Psychological Well-Being: What Does the Empirical Literature Say? *Roeper Review, 22*(1), 10–17, 1999.

Neihart, M. Gifted Children with Asperger's Syndrome. *Gifted Child Quarterly, 44*(4), 222–230, 2000.

Neihart, Maureen et al. (Eds.). *The Social and Emotional Development of Gifted Children: What Do We Know?* Waco, TX: Prufock Press, 2002.

Olenchak, F. R. Talent Development. *Journal of Secondary Gifted Education, 5*(3), 40–52, 1994.

Peters, Daniel. *Make Your Worrier a Warrior: A Guide to Conquering Your Child's Fears.* Scottsdale, AZ: Great Portland Press, 2013.

Peters, R. *Laying Down the Law: The 25 Laws of Parenting to Keep Your Kids on Track, Out of Trouble, and (Pretty Much) Under Control.* New York: Rodale/St. Martin's Press, 2003.

Piechowski, M. Emotional Development and Emotional Giftedness. In *Handbook of Gifted Education,* edited by N. Colangelo and G. A. Davis (pp. 285–306). Boston: Allyn and Bacon, 1991.

Reis, S. M, and McCoach, D. B. The Underachievement of Gifted Students: What Do We Know and Where Do We Go? *Gifted Child Quarterly, 44*(3), 152–170, 2000.

Renzulli, J. S. *Systems and Models for Developing Programs for the Gifted and Talented.* Mansfield Center, CT: Creative Learning Press, 1986.

Rimm, S. B. Family Environments of Underachievement of Gifted Students: What Do We Know and Where Do We Go? *Gifted Child Quarterly, 32*(4), 353–395, 1988.

Rimm, S. B. *Why Bright Kids Gets Poor Grades, and What You Can Do about It.* New York: Crown, 1995.

Rivero, L. *Creative Home Schooling: A Resource for Smart Families.* Scottsdale, AZ: Great Potential Press, 2002.

Roeper, A. *Selected Writing and Speeches.* Minneapolis: Free Spirit, 1995.

Roeper, A. *The Eye of the Beholder: A Guided Journey to the Essence of a Child.* Scottsdale, AZ: Great Potential Press, 2007.

Ruf, Deborah. *Losing Our Minds: Gifted Children Left Behind.* Scottsdale, AZ: Great Potential Press, 2005.

Seligman, M. E. P. *The Optimistic Child: A Proven Program to Safeguard Children against Depression and Build Lifelong Resilience.* New York: Harper Collins, 1995.

Siegle, D., and Hartzel, M. *Parenting from the Inside Out: 10th ed.: How Self Understanding Can Help You Raise Children.* New York: Tarcher, 2013.

Siegle, Del. *The Underachieving Gifted Child: Recognizing, Understanding, and Reversing Underachievement.* Waco, TX: Prufrock Press, 2012.

Siegle, Del. *The Underachieving Child: Recognizing, Understanding, and Reviewing Underachievement.* Waco, TX: Prufrock Press, 2013.

Silverman, L. K. The Second Child Syndrome. *Mensa Bulletin, 320,* 18–20, 1988.

Silverman, L. K. *Counseling the Gifted and Talented.* Denver, CO: Love, 1993.

Silverman, L. K. The Gifted Individual. In *Counseling the Gifted and Talented,* edited by L. Silverman (pp. 3–28). Denver, CO: Love, 1993.

Silverman, L. K. The Construct of Asynchronous Development. *Peabody Journal of Education,* 72(3–4), 36–58, 1997.

Silverman, L. K. *Giftedness 101 Series.* New York: Springer, 2013.

Silverman, Linda, and Kearney, Kathi. Parents of the Extraordinarily Gifted. *Advanced Development Journal, 1,* 41–56, January 1989.

Silverman, Linda, and Leviton, Linda. Advice to Parents in Search of the Perfect Program. *Gifted Child Today, 14*(6), 31–34, 1991.

Smutney, Joan Franklin. *Stand Up for Your Gifted Child.* Minneapolis: Free Spirit Publishing, 2001.

Stern, D. *The Interpersonal World of the Infant: A View from Psychoanalysis and Development Psychology.* New York: Basic Books, 1985.

Socarides, D., and Stolorow, R. Affects and Self Objects. *Annual of Psychoanalysis,* 12–13, 105–119.

Sternberg, R. J., and Davidson, J. E. (Eds.). *Conceptions of Giftedness.* Cambridge: Cambridge University Press, 1986.

Sternberg, Robert. Critical Thinking: Its Nature, Measurement, and Improvement. In *Essays on the Intellect,* edited by Frances R. Link (pp. 45–65). Alexandria, VA: Association for Supervision and Curriculum Development, 1985.

Sternberg, Robert (Ed.). *Handbook of Creativity.* Cambridge: Cambridge University Press, 1999.

Streznewski, M. K. *Gifted Grown-Ups: The Mixed Blessings of Extraordinary Potential.* New York: Wiley and Sons, 1999.

Tolan, Stephanie. *Is It a Cheetah?* Hollingworth Center, 1997 (cited May 29, 2002). Available at www//ditd.org/cybersource /record.

Tucker, B., and Hafenstein, N. L. Psychological Intensities in Young Gifted Children. *Gifted Child Quarterly, 41*(3), 66–75, 1997.

Webb, J., Amend, E. R., Webb, N. E., Goerss, J., Belgian P., and Olenchak, F. R. *Misdiagnosis and Dual Diagnosis of Gifted Children and Adults: ADHD, Bipolar, OCD, Asperger's, Depression and Other Disorders.* Scottsdale, AZ: Great Potential Press, 2005.

Webb, J. T., and DeVries, A. R. *Gifted Parent Groups: The SENG Model.* Scottsdale, AZ: Great Potential Press, 1998.

Webb, James T. A. *Searching for Meaning: Idealism, Bright Minds, Disillusionment, and Hope.* Scottsdale, AZ: Great Potential Press, 2013.

Willas, C., and Turnbull, J. *Infant/Child Mental Health: Early Interception and Relationship-Based Theories.* New York: Thornton, 2009.

Winner, Ellen. Exceptionally High Intelligence and Schooling. *American Psychologist, 52,* 1070–1081, 1997.

Winnicott, D. The Theory of Parent-Infant Relationships. *International Journal of Psychoanalysis, 41,* 89–97, 1960.

Winnicott, D. The Mother-Infant Experience of Mutuality. In *Parenthood: Its Psychology and Psychopathology,* edited by Anthony and Benedek (pp. 245–256). Boston: Little Brown, 1970.

Young, K. Tips for Parents: Parenting in the Digital Age. Available at www.davidson institute.com.

Index

About the Author

BARBARA KLEIN completed a PhD in clinical psychology at California Graduate Institute in 1985. She received a doctorate in education from the University of Southern California in 1982. Klein has worked with children and their families in clinical practice since 1986. She is the author of eight books about developmental psychology, twins, and schooling. Currently, her consulting practice is dedicated to the special needs of gifted children and their parents.

33666501357593

HQ773.5 .K538 2015
Klein, Barbara Schave
The challenges of gifted
 children
                                / 2/15

Evelyn S. Field Library
Raritan Valley Community College
118 Lamington Road
North Branch, NJ 08876-1265